DISCOVERIN
ECONOMICS
MACROECONOMICS

Edited by David Gray

AUTHORS
Kevin Berry
Fran Smith
Hugh Milroy
David Gray
Jim Nettleship
Russ Moon
David Harston
Ron Spicer
David Lee
Mike Southworth

CPL

Causeway Press Limited

Causeway Press Limited
PO Box 13, Ormskirk, Lancs. L39 5HP
©Causeway Press Limited 1988
1st Impression 1988
Reprinted 1989, 1990, 1991

British Library Cataloguing in Publication Data

Discovering economics.
  Book 1: Macroeconomics
  1. Economics
  I. Gray, David, 1957–
  330

  ISBN 0–946183–41–4

Typesetting by Chapterhouse, Formby.
Printed and bound by The Alden Press, Oxford.

CONTENTS

Introduction

ACKNOWLEDGEMENTS

The authors and publishers are grateful to all those who permitted the use of copyright material in this book. Due acknowledgement has been made to each source under the appropriate piece of data. Data from the Department of Employment, DHSS, CSO and HMSO reproduced with the permission of the Controller, Her Majesty's Stationery Office, Crown copyright reserved. Data from the National Westminster Bank edited by Dr. S. Reardon.

The publishers wish to thank the following for the use of materials: The Guardian (photographs in data 1.2, 2.20, 9.8 and cover), The Ford Motor Company (photographs in data 7.10 and cover), SNCF/CAV (photograph in data 3.19), Steve Robertson (photographs in data 8.17), Wolver-hampton Council (photograph in data 4.7), Andrew Allen Associates (graph in data 9.29 and cover), A. C. Evans (cartoons in data 8.7, 8.25 and 8.27), Hoskyns Group plc/Melvyn Bagshaw (cartoon in data 6.9). Cartoons in data 5.26 and 9.17 reproduced by permission of Punch.

Non-original artwork and cover design by Windridge and Jane.

INTRODUCTION

A new approach to A and A/S level economics

How can I discover the theories and ideas in economics for myself? How can theories be made relevant and how can they be explained using everyday examples? How can I practise the skills required for the examination and also build up a knowledge of the subject?

Discovering Economics, Macroeconomics answers these questions. It concentrates on ten main areas of economics and enables you to discover answers by working through a series of questions/activities based on relevant data. Teachers can use the book as an aid to classroom teaching and students can use the book for self-study. Each chapter is organised in the following way:

Section/Hypothesis

Each section begins with an hypothesis, eg Free trade gives a greater output of goods and services, and a higher standard of living than trade protection. By examining all of the data in each section you should be in a position to support or reject the hypothesis. The ten sections concentrate on major areas of macroeconomics, especially those found in examinations.

Task

Each section contains a number of tasks which outline and explain major theories and debates, eg To discover the cause of inflation. Each task could be completed in isolation. However by attempting all tasks in sequence you should be able to support or reject the hypothesis. The questions and data in each task form a body of knowledge and understanding which could be used as the basis of essay answers and revision notes.

Activity

In order to complete a task you must work through a number of linked activities. Activities make use of relevant data. By investigating the data you should discover ideas for yourself. Activities can be attempted individually, or in groups. In some cases group work has been emphasised by the author. The skills required for data response questions will be developed as you work through the activities.

The authors have taken care to provide varied and relevant data, which will enable all questions to be answered. The emphasis throughout the book is placed on discovery learning. The data has, in the main, been reproduced in its original form with the source quoted underneath. The majority of the data is taken from recent experience preceding the publication of this book. However, in certain cases, data from an earlier period has been used as it clearly illustrates a phenomena that was occurring at that time.

SECTION 1 National Income

HYPOTHESIS	National income statistics, by themselves, do not provide an adequate or accurate measure of an economy's standard of living.

How do we know we are getting richer? How rich are we, as individuals, compared to others in society? How far up the international league table are we as a nation? These questions, and others like them, concern the standard of living, or the economic health of the economy. In order to answer such questions, economists need information. But what information is appropriate, and how accurate is that information? The passage in data 1.1 by David Lipsey seems to suggest people's living standards rose significantly in the 1970s.

1.1

It may seem hard to credit that the 1970s were a decade of unparalleled affluence, according to an official survey of 15,000 British households published last week. This was the decade when we broke with the hallowed tradition of the ice-cold bedroom – by the end of the period, nearly three in five British homes had central heating. Gone too was the traipse across the yard to the loo – the fate of five million people in 1971 but for only one million by 1980. We became cleaner – the number of people without a washing machine fell by a third, and the proportion without a vacuum cleaner fell by a half. More people had phones, cars, colour TVs...

Source: David Lipsey *The Sunday Times* 1980

TASK 1 To evaluate the need for information on the national income.

ACTIVITY 1

Most textbooks begin a discussion of the standard of living by considering national income statistics. These are figures drawn up by government statisticians. Thus, we are confronted with aggregated sums for consumers' expenditure, government expenditure, investment, imports and exports, outputs and incomes. Though very useful, these statistics are only a part of the standard of living story.

Consider data 1.2. Does a high national income necessarily mean a high standard of living?

National income is the monetary value of all the goods and services becoming available to the citizens of an economy during a year from economic activity.

1.2

ACTIVITY 2

Look at data 1.3.

A   From the newspaper headlines make a list of the information you think you would need to make an assessment of Britain's 'economic health' or standard of living.

B   Where might you find such information?

C   What might be some of the problems in gathering such information?

D   Alongside each item on your list of information suggest why that piece of information is important and what aspects of Britain's standard of living it illustrates?

Non-oil import penetration

Import volumes as a proportion of total spending

Higher trade deficit forecast by CBI

By Steve Levinson
Economics Correspondent

Reduced growth faces Britain within two years

Economy about to peak, says bank

More jobs on the way as output hits high ground

Inflation fears send stocks tumbling

CBI FORECASTS

Deficit worsens as imports hit record

Fears of overheated economy re-emerge as shares slide in City

Retail sales boom rolls on

Source: *The Guardian, The Independent*

TASK 2 To discover how national income is measured.

Economists try to make sense of economic information by constructing simple models of the economy, designed to show the relationships between the various parts. From these models it is possible to analyse problems and make predictions based on past events. A study of the national income involves the construction of one such model – the circular flow of income model – and national income accounting is the assigning of monetary values to variables within that model.

ACTIVITY 1

In data 1.4 three points are indicated – X, Y and Z – on the circular flow diagram. Each point represents a location within the model where economists take a 'snapshot' measure of the activity in the economy. Which point should be labelled national **income**, which point national **output** and which national **expenditure**?

Households

Overseas

Z   Factor payments   Factor services   Goods and services   Y   Payment for goods and services

Government

X

Firms

Factor services–Land, labour, capital, enterprise
Factor payments–rent, wages, profit, interest

The circular flow of income shows the real and money flows between the four sectors — households, firms, the government and the rest of the world – of a simple economic model.

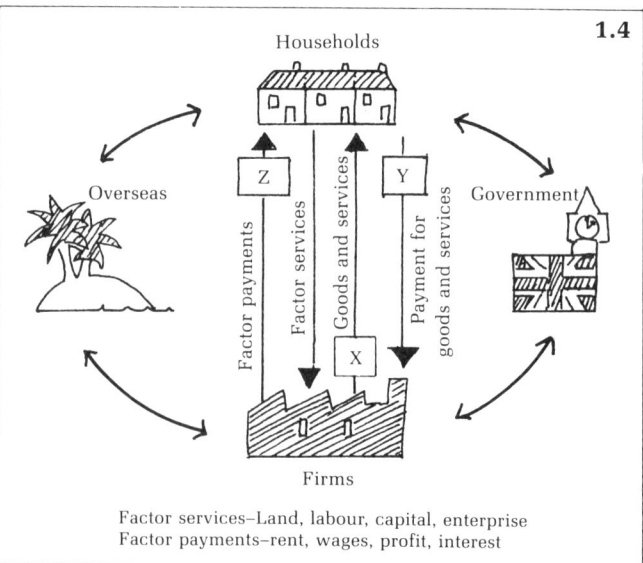

ACTIVITY 2
Using data 1.4, 1.5, and 1.6 explain the phrase: 'One person's spending is another person's income.'

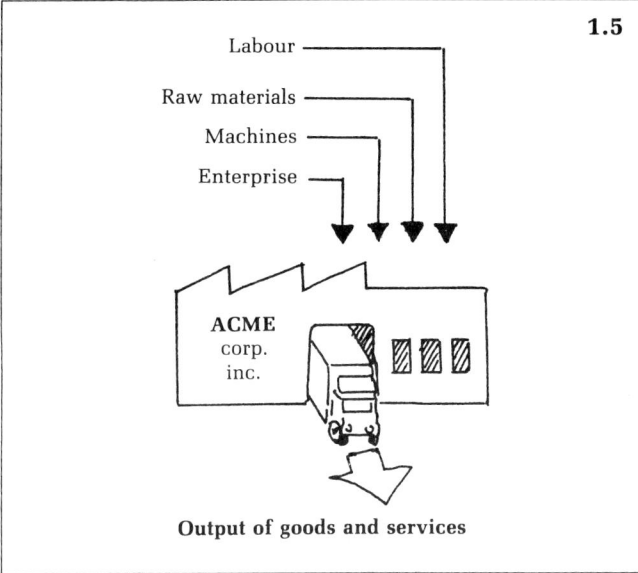

1.5

Output of goods and services

1.6.
National income can be measured in three ways.
National income: The monetary value of all the rewards to the factors of production that add value to the production of goods and services.
National output: The monetary value of all the final production of goods and services of all enterprises.
National expenditure: The monetary value of the sum of all spending on output of finished goods.

ACTIVITY 3
Data 1.7 shows a simplified set of national income statistics. Each measure gives a figure for gross domestic product (GDP).

A Draw a circular flow diagram similar to that in data 1.4.

B Allocate each item to one of the four sectors – households, firms, government or overseas.

C Why, in our simple model, must national income = national expenditure = national output? Do you think that the figures will always balance in the UK accounts? Briefly explain your answer.

1.7

National Income, Expenditure and Output figures for United Country, 198X

OUTPUT		INCOME		EXPENDITURE	
Primary Sector	49	From Employment	132	Consumers' Expenditure	213
Construction	19	Profits	152	Govt. Expenditure	74
Manufacturing	86	Rent	67	Investment	60
All Services	197			+ Exports	102
				– Imports	98
National Output	351	National Income	351	National Expenditure	351

10   Discovering Economics

TASK 3 To discover the adjustments made to overcome national income measurement problems.

Many students are worried by the terminology used in the official statistics and in trying to get to grips with each item in turn, lose sight of the purpose of the process. All we are trying to do, at the end of the day, is measure the value of the goods and services that become available to the citizens of an economy during a time period. To give an accurate picture of that activity we must do more than was implied in task 2, since we must take into account certain events that happen in the real economy. What adjustments do we need to make?

ACTIVITY 1
Data 1.8 illustrates a potential measurement problem – double counting. Explain why national income is £560 and not £1,210 in this example.

1.8

Assume a landowner inherits a piece of wooded land. He cuts down the trees and sells them to a timber merchant who cuts and finishes the timber before selling it to a carpenter.

The carpenter makes coffee tables and sells them to a furniture retailer who in turn sells the finished product to the consumer.

When measuring the value of output we must either measure the **final** value of output or the **value added** at each stage of production, otherwise we will count the value of intermediate output more than once – thus **double counting**.

STAGES OF PRODUCTION	VALUE OF SALES (£)	VALUE ADDED (£)
Landowner sells trees	100	100
Timber merchant sells cut wood	200	100
Carpenter sells coffee tables	350	150
Retailer sells tables to consumers	560	210
TOTAL VALUE OF SALES	£1210	TOTAL VALUE ADDED £560

ACTIVITY 2
Data 1.9 illustrates the problem of transfer payments.

A   What do you think a transfer payment is? Give some examples.

B   If national income can be measured as the reward to factors of production which add to the total value of output, is it, in this case, £100 or £130? Explain your answer.

1.9

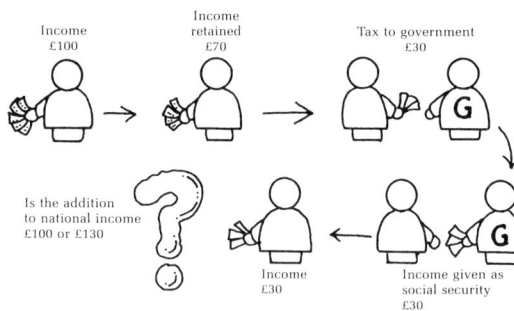

ACTIVITY 3

Data 1.10 illustrates the essential difference between a **factor cost** and a **market price** measure of economic transactions.

A Which of the two measures do you consider to be the better indicator of the value of economic activity?

B What two rules could you write to explain how to change
- a factor cost measure to one at market prices
- a measure at market prices to one at factor cost?

1.10

A £3.50 bottle of wine includes tax duties of £1.90.

The market price you pay £3.50
Factor cost to produce £1.60

A 25p bottle of milk includes a subsidy of 4p.

The market price you pay 25p
Factor cost to produce 29p

ACTIVITY 4

During any one year, investment or **gross fixed capital formation** takes place. Some of that investment, however, just replaces existing assets and therefore in itself does not add to the goods and services becoming available to the citizens of the economy. Hence we calculate national income as a net (of replacement investment which is often called **capital consumption** or **depreciation**) as well as a gross figure.

Examine data 1.11.

What rule could you write to explain how to change a gross measure of national income into a net measure?

1.11

How capital is consumed

The resale value of a photocopying machine. Initial purchase price £750.

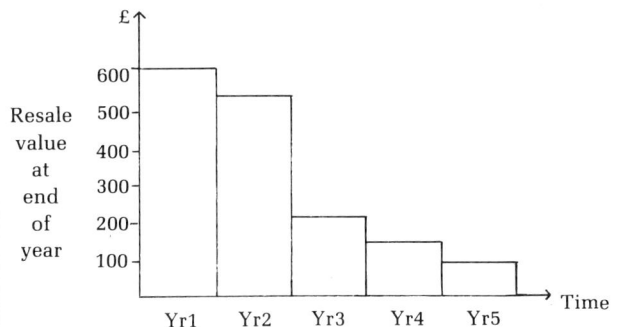

If the company decides to replace the photocopying machine the value of the new one, up to £750 will be classified as replacement investment. If the company decides to spend more than £750, the difference will be classified as net investment.

ACTIVITY 5

Foreign individuals and companies receive interest, profits and dividends from investments they have made in subsidiaries in the UK; likewise UK firms and individuals earn income on their interests in overseas operations. This is illustrated in data 1.12. Why must we make a **net property income from abroad** adjustment to arrive at an accurate measure of national income?

1.12

Speakers raise jobs volume

ONE OF Europe's leading manufacturers and designers of loudspeakers for the original equipment market is embarking on a major expansion programme which will create 300 jobs at Bridgend in South Wales.

The WDA is building a £1 million, 49,500 sq. ft. factory on a 3.8-acre green-field site for Electro Acoustic Industries. The purpose-built factory has been tailored to meet the company's specialised manufacturing requirements and can be extended in phases as the company grows.

Electro Acoustic Industries (ELAC), was established in 1946 and manufactures a range of components for the international electronics industry. Speaker units made by ELAC are used extensively in industrial and consumer markets and the company supplies its speaker units as original equipment to much of the European motor industry.

The company has an extensive research and development facility and, apart from its close involvement with car manufacturers, has expanded strongly into other specialised markets, notably telecommunications and hi-fi.

Major telecommunications customers include British Telecom, GEC, ITT/STC, Marconi, Plessey and Pye. ELAC supplies nearly every British major hi-fi manufacturer with component loudspeaker units. Above, an impression of the completed building.

Source: *Welsh Development Agency News* May 1986

ACTIVITY 6

Using the statistics in data 1.13 calculate the following:

A   GDP at market prices

B   GDP at factor cost

C   GNP at factor cost

D   National Income (NNP at factor cost)
Use data 1.14 to help you.

1.13

Item	£ billion
Consumers' expenditure	182
Government expenditure	66
Gross domestic capital formation	50
Exports of goods and services	80
Imports of goods and services	77
Taxes on expenditure less subsidies	44
Net property income from abroad	2
Capital consumption	36

Source: Adapted from *National Income and Expenditure* HMSO 1983

1.14

The three approaches to measuring national income

All expenditures + Exports − Imports	$= \text{GDP}_{MP} \; {}^{-\text{Tax}}_{+\text{sub}} = \text{GDP}_{FC} + \text{NPIA} = \text{GNP}_{FC} - \text{depreciation} =$	National income (NNP)

All incomes − stock appreciation + residual error	$= \text{GDP}_{FC} + \text{NPIA} =$

All outputs (including adjustment to avoid double counting) + residual error

GDP = Gross domestic product
GNP = Gross national product
NNP = Net national product
NPIA = Net property income from abroad
MP = Market prices
FC = Factor cost

Stock appreciation: Stocks of raw materials, and finished goods may go up in value during the course of a year due to inflation. In measuring the national income we must only record physical changes in stocks.

Residual Error: As we have seen (task 2) all three measures of national income should sum to the same figure. In reality they do not and this is not surprising given the many sources of information and the thousands of calculations involved. The residual error is an accounting item, rather like the balancing item in the balance of payments accounts to ensure that the three methods of measuring national income produce the same aggregate sum.

ACTIVITY 7

Data 1.15 shows the national income for the UK for 1985. The level of depreciation in the economy and the net value of income earned abroad are shown separately. Calculate the national income for the UK in 1985.

1.15

The income approach

	£million
Income from employment	195350
Income from self-employment	29859
Gross trading profits	52977
Gross trading surplus of public corporations	7106
Gross trading surplus of general government enterprises	264
Rent	20541
Imputed charge for consumption of non-trading capital	2681
Total domestic income	308778
Less stock appreciation	− 3037
Residual error	− 3276
GDP at factor cost	302465

The expenditure approach

	£million
Consumers' expenditure	213208
General govt. final consumption	74012
Gross domestic fixed capital formation	60118
Value of physical increase in stocks	528
Exports	102304
Less imports	− 98603
GDP at market prices	351567
Less indirect taxes plus subsidies	− 49102
GDP at factor cost	302465

Net property income from abroad	£ 3400m
Capital consumption	− £41846m

The output approach

	£million
Agric., forest, fishing	5485
Energy & water	34335
Manufacturing	76800
Construction	18651
Distribution, hotels etc.	40384
Communication	8044
Transport	12913
Banking and finance services	42473
Ownership of dwellings	17775
Public admin. & defence	21599
Education & health	26187
Other services	17978
Total	322624
Adjustment for double counting	− 16883
Residual error	− 3276
GDP at factor cost	302465

Source: *National Income and Expenditure* HMSO 1986

TASK 4 To evaluate the usefulness of national income statistics as indicators of living standards.

You will have noticed already how complicated a process it is compiling national income statistics, and you will no doubt appreciate the potential for inaccuracy. Furthermore, you may already be sceptical of the usefulness of the figures as a measure of standards of living.

ACTIVITY 1

A   Why would it be inaccurate to conclude from data 1.16 that UK citizens were almost three times richer in 1985 than they were in 1975?

B   How could the government overcome this problem of interpretation?

1.16

UK/NNP (£million)

1975	85,060
1985	264,019

Prices increased by average annual rate of 12 per cent between 1975 and 1985.

Source: Adapted from *National Income and Expenditure* HMSO

Of course, it is possible to overcome the effects of inflation, by indexation – by calculating the current price measures of national income above, thus producing a constant price measure in the prices of the base year. Only this adjustment overcomes the inflation problem so beware using current price figures when analysing national income statistics for an economy over time.

ACTIVITY 2
Examine data 1.17.

Even if changes in real national income are considered rather than changes in purely money terms, they still may not accurately reflect changes in living standards if there have been significant changes in population during the time period under consideration. This may not present a problem when analysing the UK case, since recent population growth has been small, but may be most important when considering economic growth in Third World countries, for instance.

What was the change in real national income per head (or **per capita**) for Anycountry between 1997 and 1998?

1.17

Population and real NNP for Anycountry, 1997–1998

YEAR	NATIONAL INCOME (£million)	POPULATION
1997	600	100000
1998	660	120000

ACTIVITY 3
Reference only to the bald statistics also gives little insight into the sorts of goods and services becoming available to the citizens of an economy. Thus they do not tell us about the proportion of total output and consumption that is made up of economic bads.

Look at data 1.18 and 1.19.

A Make a list of economic bads.

B In what ways might the production of economic bads actually lower a country's standard of living?

C Why might the output of and expenditure on arms and tobacco be considered 'good for the national wealth, but bad for the national health'?

1.18

1.19

● DEFENCE contractors are anxiously waiting for Whitehall to decide if Britain is to join seven other Nato countries in developing the frigate of the 1990s, codenamed NFR 90.

All eight nations have until October 21 to make a financial commitment to proceed with the design stage. So far only Britain has failed to signal a readiness to go ahead.

Source: *The Observer* September 1987

ACTIVITY 4
Read data 1.20.

Official statistics inevitably omit a proportion of economic activity that takes place.

A Make a list of possible 'black economy' activities.

B Why is the existence of the 'black economy' important for national income measurement?

C Should a teenager, receiving £1 from his/her parents for cleaning the family car, be recorded in the national income accounts? Explain your answer.

1.20

THE TREASURY FISH THAT GOT AWAY IS PROBABLY BIGGER IN THE STORY THAN IN THE WATER

Victor Keegan

Few subjects generate such a head of steam from such a paucity of facts as the so-called "black economy" of moonlighting and tax avoidance. It has been estimated to account for anything from 2 to 15 per cent of the entire economy. Some see it as evidence of the moral decline of the nation. Others hail it as the source of ultimate salvation—a resurgence of entrepreneurial activity sheltered from the disincentive influence of the tax man. It is even seen as a harbinger of fundamental economic change—a slow relapse into the "informal economy" of the earlier centuries after 200 years or so of formal activity.

There is only one important ingredient which black economy stories lack: reliable information. Nobody actually knows how big the black economy is at the moment, let alone how large it was 10 or 20 years ago.

Most estimates of its size derive from dubious deductions from national incomes statistics which are themselves prone to errors almost as large as the estimates of the informal economy. Some of the higher estimates are particularly suspect.

Professor Edgar L. Fiege, the US economist, reckons that black activity accounts for at least 15 per cent of the UK national income—twice the size of the guess of $7\frac{1}{2}$ per cent made by the head of the Inland Revenue. If the higher calculation were true it would mean that every household in the UK spent about £1,500 a year on black economy goods. Is that really plausible?

Many people think the black economy is bigger than it is simply because they now own their own houses (and therefore come into contact with the "black" jobs associated with house improvement) whereas 20 years ago they didn't own a house and so hardly ever came across such activity. The black economy may have risen as a proporton of their outgoings but it does not follow that it is growing for the nation as a whole.

As the Institute for Fiscal Studies observed, the black economy can be large enough to yield several billions of pounds of rich anecdotes without adding up to a significant percentage of the economy. The case that higher taxes have produced a sharp growth in the black economy is not yet proven.

Source: *The Guardian* May 17 1982

1.21

	1974	1979	1984
Dwellings per '000 pop.	349	370	381
TV licences per '000 pop.	308	327	330
Private cars (licences) per '000	244	261	283
Fridges percentage pop owning	82	83	94
Pupils per teacher	20.8	19.1	17.8
Civil servants per '000	12.3	13.0	11.1
Real personal disposable income per head, 1984 prices	£3422	£3811	£3898
Telephones per '000	337	440	520

Source: *Britain: The Economy in Figures* Lloyds Bank 1985

Britain v Italy: who has the mostest?

Has Italy overtaken Britain as the fifth most important economy in the world? The Italians seem to think so. They call it *Il Surpasso*. Whether their belief is supported by the evidence depends upon which figures you use. All this jostling for economic positioning may not seem to matter to you, but it definitely does to those in politics, since it determines who gets invited to the big international meetings.

The Italians are convinced they're fifth on the economic ladder: the Milan Stock Exchange is booming, and the whole economy is solid, they say. The British are equally sure that the Italians have got their sums wrong. The Italians adjust GDP per capita for the two countries for relative currency movements against the dollar and come out, they claim, a fist full of lira up, the Brits disagree. Furthermore, the Italians say that their black economy adds an additional 12 per cent–15 per cent to push their economy into fourth place in division one. And when you take into account those factors not normally considered then they excitedly claim they're streets ahead (see 'who has the most' table).

Who's who in the world rankings matters when you consider that the Group of Five big economies meet regularly to make policy decisions that affect the rest of the industrialised world. But this is not the end of the story; a neutral Frenchman at the Paris-based OECD says of the recent Italian claims: 'Maybe the Italian economy is about as strong as the UK's but, the Italians have boomed on a mountain of debt, and it could all collapse. Sterling is still a strong international currency, London is a more important international financial centre than is Milan, and the British still do have some oil.'

1.22

Exchange rates

Dec. 1986 £1 = L1980
Mar. 1987 £1 = L2110

Where they rank in the world

100 = Average income per head in Europe

Portugal — 51.3; Greece; Ireland; Spain; Italy 92.4; Belgium 106.6; Great Britain; Netherlands; France; W. Germany; Denmark; Luxembourg; Japan 113.8; United States 160.7

Who has the most?

	Italy	UK
Cars	67	58
Washing machines	81	77
Dishwashers	14	3
TVs	24	34
Running water	75	100
Doctors	3.6	0.5

All figures per 100 families, except doctors, per 1000 people.

Source: EEC

Source: Adapted from *The Sunday Times* March 15 1987

SECTION 2   Economic Growth

HYPOTHESIS	Economic growth is both achievable and desirable.

Economic growth is usually explained in ordinary language as an increase in the general standard of living of a country. If national income or gross national product has increased then economic growth has occurred. Most economists believe that some growth is a good thing, but some others feel that pursuing growth above all things can impose a heavy cost on society. This debate is outlined in data 2.1–2.4.

2.1

WHAT GROWTH MEANS

Hours of work*		Holidays of 4 weeks +		Life expectancy at 1 year (men)	
1970	1985	1970	1985	1901	1983
47	41.9	7%	99%	55 (years)	71.2 (years)

*male manual workers

Households with car		Households with 'phone		Households with central heating	
1973	1985	1973	1985	1974	1984
54%	62%	45%	81%	39%	60%

Source: *Social Trends* HMSO 1983

2.2

For example, having established by his purely quantitative methods that the gross national product of a country has risen by, say, 5 per cent, the economist... is unwilling, and generally unable to face the question of whether this is to be taken as a good or a bad thing... growth of GNP must be a good thing, (he thinks), irrespective of what has grown and who, if anyone, has benefited. The idea that there could be... unhealthy growth, disruptive or destructive growth is to him a perverse idea which should not be allowed to surface.

Source: F. F. Schumacher *Small is Beautiful* Sphere Books Ltd London 1974

2.3

I think there is enough evidence from the data to suggest that increasing GDP numbers do tell us something about... increasing welfare. It seems to me inconceivable that one can seriously argue that longer life expectancy, shorter working hours, longer holidays, greater freedom of choice and travel, more telephones and more central heating reduce welfare rather than increase it.

Source: C. Huhne *The Guardian* December 29 1983

2.4

Source: J. F. Bartellier *Is Anybody Out There?* Free Association Books London 1984

TASK 1   To discover what is meant by economic growth.

Economic growth can be explained and illustrated using a production possibility curve.

ACTIVITY 1
Consider data 2.5 and 2.6.

A   What might be meant by an increase in productive potential?

B   Explain, using the definitions in data 2.6, what represents economic growth on the diagram.

C   Try to decide whether position X or Z would result in greater long-term growth. Justify your answer using the definitions in data 2.6.

D   Using the explanation of the curve give reasons why a movement from position P to Y may not represent growth.

2.5

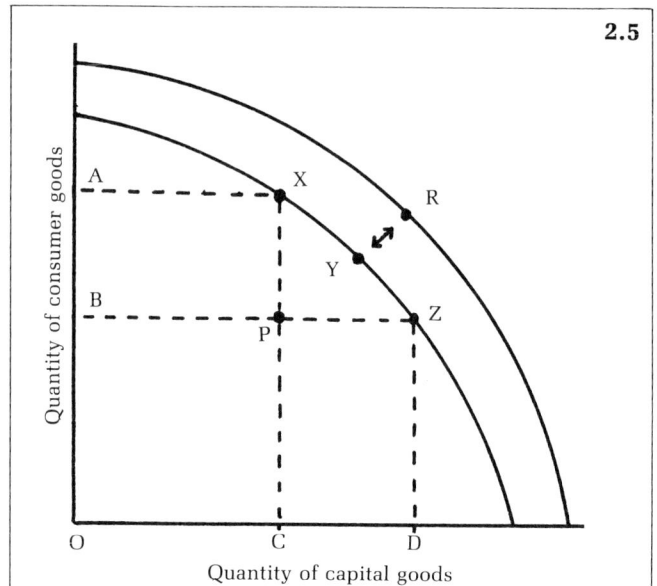

This diagram illustrates a production possibility curve. It shows all the possible combinations of goods an economy could produce working at full capacity, ie no idle resources. It therefore represents maximum possible combinations.

If this economy was producing OC capital goods it could only produce OA consumer goods. Any increase in the production of capital goods (OC to OD) would require a sacrifice (opportunity cost) of consumer goods (OA to OB).

2.6

Economic growth – An increase in the goods and services produced/an increase in productive potential.

Capital goods – goods that are themselves produced and are used to make other goods, eg machines.

Consumer goods – goods that provide immediate satisfaction.

TASK 2   To examine the UK's growth performance over time, and relative to other developed countries.

Though, over time, Britain has had a growing economy, her performance relatively speaking has caused much concern.

ACTIVITY 1

Consider data 2.7. What has happened to UK growth since 1981? Use data 2.8 to explain why this might have happened.

2.8

Year	Output per person employed (Index nos) 1980:100	Gross domestic* fixed capital formation (£ million)
1981	101.8	30.692
1982	105.8	32.207
1983	109.8	33.247
1984	111.3	36.598
1985	113.6	37.376

*Broadly speaking investment
Source: Adapted from *UK Economy* 11th Edition Edited by A.J. Artis
Weidenfeld and Nicolson London 1986

2.7

British Industrial Performance NEDC

Recent UK experience
GDP: change from previous year

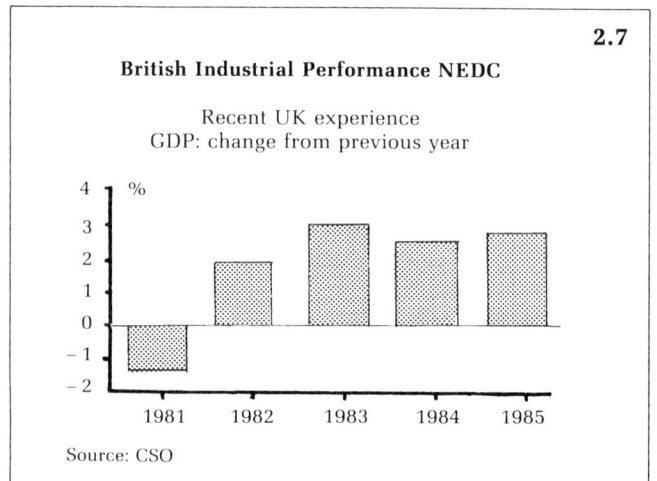

Source: CSO

ACTIVITY 2
Consider data 2.9.

A Draw up a table of the information contained.

B What might be problematic about measuring growth in percentage terms?

C Why might growth be measured at 'constant 1980 prices'?

D Using the information in data 2.10–2.12 suggest reasons for the UK's relative performance.

2.9

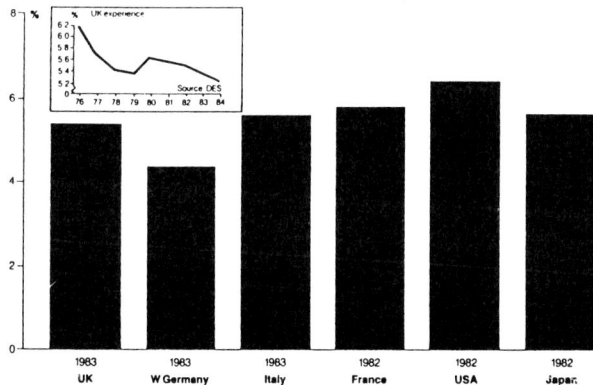

Growth: Average annual increase in real GDP
Constant 1980 prices

Source: OECD

2.10

Production can be increased in 5 different ways:

1 Increase the productivity or supply of labour.

2 Increase the productivity or supply of capital.

3 Technological innovation (which increases the output of productive resources).

4 Eliminate waste, fully employ labour, capital and raw materials.

5 Combine resources more efficiently – use labour and capital in more efficient combinations.

Source: Adapted from J. K. Galbraith *The Affluent Society* Pelican Harmondsworth 1962

2.11

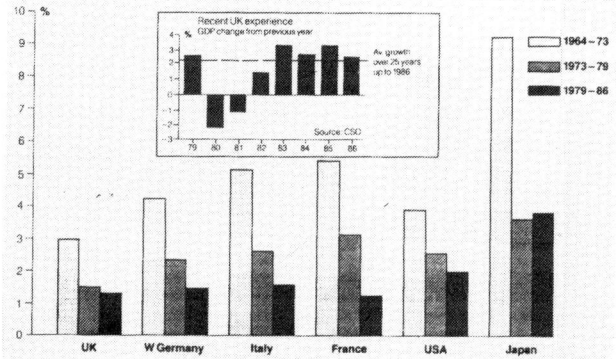

Public education and related expenditure: Percentage of GDP

Source: Department of Education and Science

2.12
Total factor productivity: Annual average growth rate

	Pre 1973	1973–79	1979–86	1986–89
United States	+ 1.5	− 0.1	+ 0.1	+ 0.2
Japan	+ 6.3	+ 1.8	+ 1.7	+ 1.9
Germany	+ 2.6	+ 1.8	+ 0.8	+ 0.7
France	+ 4.3	+ 2.1	+ 1.2	+ 1.3
Italy	+ 4.8	+ 1.6	+ 0.7	+ 0.9
UK	+ 1.9	+ 0.2	+ 1.0	+ 2.0
OECD Average	+ 2.9	+ 0.7	+ 0.6	+ 0.7

Source: OECD

TASK 3   To consider how growth is achieved, ie the sources of economic growth.

ACTIVITY 1
Consider data 2.13–2.15.

A   In the light of the definition, explain why investment is important in terms of increasing a nation's productive capacity.

B   What opportunity cost might be involved in high levels of investment? Refer to data 2.5 to help you.

C   Examine the link between investment and growth using the figures in data 2.15.

2.13

INVESTMENT – The process of creating capital.

2.14

The production function can be written as:

Output = f (capital, labour, land, raw materials, technical knowledge).

The production function shows the maximum output that can be produced using specified quantities of inputs, given the existing technical knowledge.

Increases in potential output can be traced to increases in inputs of the factors of production – land, labour, capital, raw materials – or to technical advances allowing the existing factors to produce a higher level of output.

Source: *Economics* Begg, Fischer and Dornbusch McGraw-Hill Maidenhead 1984

2.15

Growth & Investment in the UK

Year	GDP at 1980 prices (£ million)	Gross Domestic Fixed Capital Formation at at 1980 prices* (£ million)
1981	19,6987	30,692
1982	19,9414	32,207
1983	20,6748	33,247
1984	21,0205	36,598
1985	21,7217	37,376

*Broadly speaking investment
Source: Adapted from *The UK Economy* Edited by A. J. Artis Weidenfeld and Nicolson London 1986

ACTIVITY 2

A   Data 2.16 represents a form of 'investment in human capital'. What effect will the statements have on economic growth?

B   List as many ways as you can of improving the quality of the labour force.

C   Consider data 2.17. Try to judge whether, and how, they would improve employment and the quality of the labour force. Give reasons to support your arguments. What problems could there be in implementing such policies?

D   Look at data 2.18 and 2.19. Explain how the YTS is designed to promote occupational mobility and, therefore, economic growth.

2.16

British dunces – no good to industry.

No dole for lazy louts.

Computers or classics? – the choice for schools.

Education – the national scandal.

2.17

JOBS AND TRAINING — WHAT THE POLITICIANS SAY

LABOUR
- statutory minimum wage.
- jobs/training for all 16 year olds.
- lower national insurance contributions for employers.

ALLIANCE
- job/training guaranteed for all unemployed.
- cut employers' insurance contributions in high unemployment areas.

TORY
- guaranteed places on YTS.
- no dole for those who say no.
- scheme places for 18–25 year olds out of work for 6–12 months.
- a place for all under 50s and 2 year jobless on government schemes.

Source: Adapted from *The Economist* May 23–29 1987

2.18

David Young, Chairman of the MSC made the following statement during a YTS launching ceremony in January 1983.
    'We have tried to do something about impediments in the labour market which have stood in the way of change. Thus we have introduced important new training measures to increase the skill and flexibility of the workforce. We have introduced measures to increase mobility.'

2.19

Occupational mobility of labour: the ability or willingness of labour to move between jobs.

ACTIVITY 3

A What do the quotes and the photograph suggest about strikes in the UK?
   Does it coincide with the statistical evidence in data 2.22?

B Suggest ways in which industrial action might affect economic growth. Use data 2.22 and 2.23 to help you.

2.20

WORKERS FAIL TO REACH AGREEMENT.

BRITAIN'S POOR STRIKE RECORD.

THE BRITISH DISEASE

2.21

2.22

DAYS OF WORK LOST PER YEAR PER EMPLOYEE BECAUSE OF INDUSTRIAL DISPUTES 1977–78

UK	0.39
GERMANY	0.06
JAPAN	0.13
FRANCE	0.22
USA	0.46
CANADA	1.01
ITALY	1.22

Source: *Current Topics in Economics and Business Studies A Summary of the UK Economy 1985/86* D. McCarthy Mentor Dublin

2.23

'Gross national product was 1 per cent less due to the loss of coal production and loss of output in industries dependent upon coal supplies for energy.'

Source: *Current Topics in Economics and Business Studies – A Summary of the UK Economy 1985/86* D. McCarthy Mentor Dublin

ACTIVITY 4

A In what ways could North Sea oil help Britain achieve economic growth?

B 'Oil decline will pose colossal strategic problems for the British economy.' Why? Do you agree? Has Britain become overly dependent on oil? Use data 2.25 to support your argument.

2.24

NORTH SEA OIL BONANZA HITS UK

Everyone knows North Sea oil will eventually run out but this fact plays little part in the current discussion of economic policy. Yet the onset of its decline is quite close . . . Oil decline will pose colossal strategic problems for the British economy. And it is these which should be dominating the discussion of economic policy.

Source: Godley & Cripps *The Guardian* March 14 1987

2.25

Balance of Trade (£ billion)

	1981	1982	1983	1984	1985
Oil Balance	+ 3.1	+ 4.6	+ 7.0	+ 7.0	+ 8.5
Non-Oil Balance	− 0.1	− 2.5	− 8.0	− 11.0	− 10.5
Visible Trade Balance	+ 3.0	+ 2.1	− 1.0	− 4.0	− 2.0

Without oil the visible deficits in recent years would have been much greater. The overall balance of payments situation in 1985 without the favourable oil balance would have been a current deficit of £4½ billion instead of a surplus of £4 billion.

Source: *Current Topics in Economics and Business Studies A Summary of the UK Economy 1985/86* D. McCarthy Mentor Dublin

ACTIVITY 5

A Try to distinguish between
  • innovation and invention.
  • product innovation and technical innovation using data 2.26.
  Illustrate with examples.

B What is the link between investment in Research & Development and growth?

C Does the evidence suggest that investment in certain areas has a greater effect on growth? Use data 2.27 and 2.28 to support your argument.

D It is often asserted that Britain develops products and other countries produce them.
  Can you think of any examples?
  Why might this happen? Does it matter?

2.26

INNOVATION

INVENTION

Source: *Hey BC* J. Hart Hodder and Stoughton London 1979

2.27

	Rates of Growth 1970–79
UK	2.2
W. Germany	2.9
Italy	3.0
France	3.9
USA	3.4
Japan	4.9

Source: Adapted from *National Accounts of OECD Countries* 1982

2.28

R&D share: R&D expenditure as a percentage of GDP

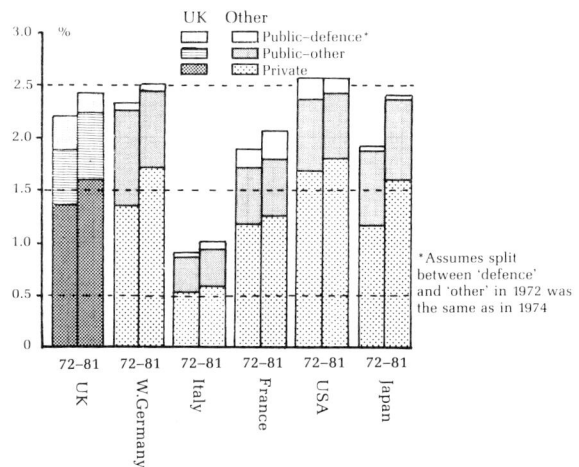

*Assumes split between 'defence' and 'other' in 1972 was the same as in 1974

Source: OECD

TASK 4   To consider whether economic growth is desirable.

ACTIVITY 1

A   Look at the cartoon – Floss National Product and extract 2.29. Explain, in terms of economic growth, what happened in Floss.

B   Using the 'Floss experience' and data 2.29 list the costs of economic growth.

2.29

Statisticians and politicians count the increasing flow of material output as a triumph of modern civilisation. Consider not the flow of output in general, but the products that it contains. You arise from your electric-blanketed bed, clean your teeth with an electric toothbrush, open with an electric tin-opener a tin of the sad remains of a once-proud orange, you eat your bread baked from super-refined and chemically refortified flour, and you climb into your car to sit in vast traffic jams on exhaust-polluted motorways. And so the day goes, with endless consumption of high technology products that give you no more real satisfaction than the simple products consumed by your grandfathers: soft woolly blankets, natural bristle toothbrushes, real oranges, old-fashioned and coarse but healthy bread, and public transport that moved on uncongested roads and gave its passengers time to chat with their neighbours, to read, and just to daydream.

Source: R. G. Lipsey *Positive Economics* Weidenfeld and Nicolson 1984 London

2.30

Source: *The New Internationalist* April 1984

ACTIVITY 2
Examine data 2.31

A From what you have learnt outline the benefits of economic growth.

B Why, does the article suggest, would some people be anti-growth?

2.31

Today, we have the best of all possible worlds. Our living standards are higher than ever before – few homes are without a video, a stereo, a colour TV or a car. Many now aspire realistically to the microwave or the compact disc player. Education is the right of all not the privilege of the few. A consumer society indeed, but who are the consumers? They are the ordinary men and women who, with higher living standards and more leisure time, reap daily benefits of sustained economic growth. Indeed, historically 'we have never had it so good'.

Agreed, there are voices of dissent, but let us examine their motives. Is it not that the general popularisation, and, more importantly, availability of many goods and services have undermined their privileged position, their élitist status? Could it be that growth, and the ensuing redistribution of income, erodes their superiority, narrows the gap between them and the common man? Is it not fear of being caught up, of not having a unique social standing that makes the few stand out against what so obviously benefits the many?

Economic growth has destroyed much of their privileged consumption position: they must now vie with the masses when visiting the world's beauty spots and be annoyed, while lounging on the terrace of their palatial mansions, by the sound of chartered jets carrying ordinary people to holidays in far places.

Source: Adapted in part from *Positive Economics* R. G. Lipsey Weidenfeld and Nicolson London 1984

ACTIVITY 3
Do you agree with the statements in data 2.32 and the comment in 2.33? Justify your answers.

'Economic growth leads to private benefits and public costs.'

2.32

'Some argue that the externalities – the side effects of growth – are so large that they swamp the benefits indicated by higher national income figures.'

Source: Adapted from an article by C. Huhne *The Guardian* December 29 1987

2.33

THE COSTS OF GROWTH?

Source: *Is Anybody Out There?* J. F. Bartellier Free Association Books London 1984

SECTION 3 Aggregate Demand

| HYPOTHESIS | There is a strong causal link between aggregate demand, national income and output. |

The basis of modern Keynesian economic theory originating from the work of John Maynard Keynes in his book *The General Theory of Employment, Interest and Money* (1936) was that output, and therefore national income is determined by the level of aggregate demand for goods and services.

Keynes' theories held sway for most of the early post-war period and became known as *demand management policies*.

Keynes argued that it was the government's job to stimulate aggregate demand if it was insufficient, or depress it if it was too great in order to raise, or lower national income. However in recent years Keynes' theory has been criticised by monetarists mainly on the grounds of 'heavy handed' use of policies and the effect of financing them on the level of inflation. This debate is examined in data 3.1–3.3.

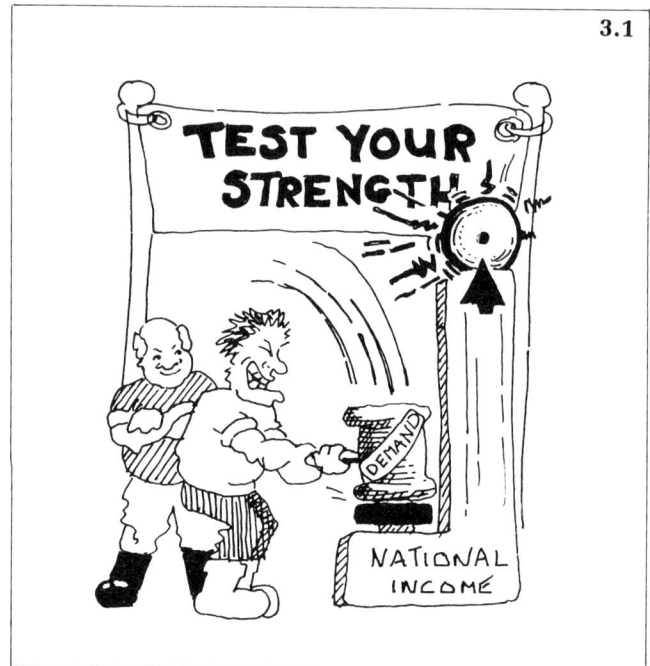

3.1

3.2

'Fiscal policy, by cutting taxes and expanding the budget deficit, is responsible for the rapid growth of output and employment... US inflation will be higher than other countries whose budget deficit is... small because the budget deficit will pump in demand even at full employment.'

Source: Geoffrey Dicks 'Does Britain need Reaganomics?' *The Guardian* February 1985

3.3

'Insufficient aggregate demand produces a gap between potential output and actual output. According to Keynes' theory the obvious remedy was to implement a stimulative fiscal and monetary policy.'

Source: J.L. Stein *Monetarists, Keynesians and The New Classical Economists* Basil Blackwell Oxford 1984

TASK 1   To discover the relationship between demand, output and income.

In a modern industrial society almost all goods are produced in advance of demand. Firms must therefore sell the goods they produce to recover the money they have already spent; they will, therefore, only produce goods which they expect to sell.

ACTIVITY 1
Examine data 3.4.

A   What has happened to demand for this record and how might record companies be expected to react?

B   What effect might the DJ's comments have on output, sales and price of the record?

C   What would happen to unsold copies of the record and what effect could this have on production of his next album?

3.4

THE WORLD GOES MAD OVER BAD!

Fans scramble for Jacko's new album

By DAVID JONES and RICK SKY

FRANTIC pop fans queued world-wide yesterday to snap up Michael Jackson's long-awaited album BAD.

First-day sales were set to smash all records as shops were besieged from the moment they opened.

Music bosses had feared fans would snub eccentric Jacko because he has gone too wacko.

But yesterday's mad scramble matched the hysteria over Thriller—Jackon's smash-hit four years ago which sold 38 million copies.

Jackson's record company CBS expected BAD to sell **150,000** copies on its first day, sending it rocketing to the top of the charts.

Blowing

And they have had orders for $2\frac{1}{4}$ **MILLION** copies.

In **BRITAIN**, jostling fans snapped up 200 copies an **HOUR** at Tower Records in London's Piccadilly.

Boss Steve Smith said: "It's crazy—as soon as we load up the shelves they empty again."

And a spokesman for Virgin Records said: "I can't remember anything like this—the album is just flying out of the store."

One devoted fan bought 15 copies.

What Britain's DJs say

Simon Bates, Radio One —

"If you're looking for something to top Thriller, you'll be disappointed."

Steve Wright, Radio One —

"The album is fairly bland; more like an album leading up to something great, not following it."

Gary Davis, Radio One —

"I've only heard it once but liked every track. It could become as infectious as Thriller."

Andy Peebles, Radio One —

"Michael set himself a big problem trying to follow Thriller, but he's done a superb job."

John Sachs, Capital Radio —

"It's very different from Thriller, and shouldn't be compared with it. It's a very good soul album."

Greg Edwards, Capital Radio —

"I've got a feeling it'll top the sales figures of Thriller."

Nicky Horne, Capital Radio —

"This is using the basis of Thriller, but it's not as thrilling. It won't be going into my CD collection."

Source: *The Sun* September 2 1987 The *Daily Mirror* September 3 1987

TASK 2   To examine the relationship between disposable income, consumption and savings.

In a 'simple economy', assuming no government sector or foreign trade, the public only have two choices of what to do with their income – they can either spend it on consumption goods or save it. Saving is a withdrawal because this part of income does not return directly to firms in the purchase of goods and services. As consumption is by far the largest element of aggregate demand it is important, therefore, to know the factors that influence how much people spend and save, and, in consequence, how the nation does so as a whole.

ACTIVITY 1

A   Using the information in data 3.5 and 3.6 prove Keynes' quote from the General Theory.

B   What do you think is meant by dissaving? Item 3.8 may help you. Try to write your own definition. In what other ways can a person dissave?

C   What effect will data 3.9 have on the consumption function?

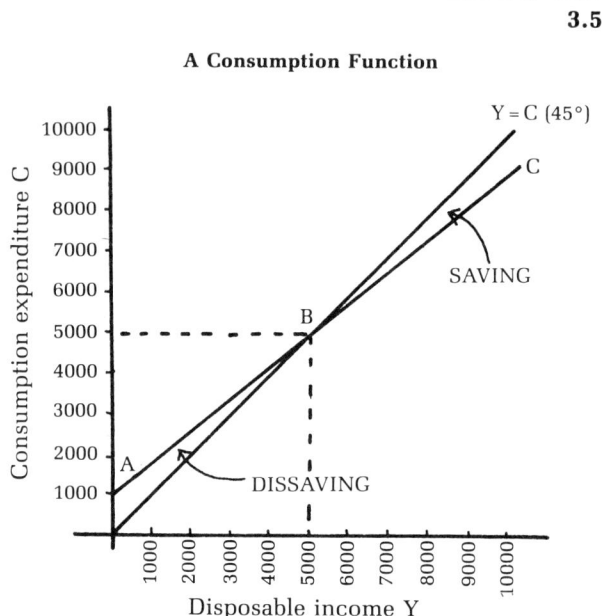

3.6

Disposable income	Planned consumption	Planned savings
0	1000	– 1000
1000	1800	– 800
2000	2600	– 600
3000	3400	– 400
4000	4200	– 200
5000	5000	0
6000	5800	200
7000	6600	400
8000	7400	600
9000	8200	800
10,000	9000	1000

3.5

A Consumption Function

The 45° line shows points where all income is spent, ie income = expenditure.

The amount of consumption at each hypothetical level of personal disposable income is known as the consumption function.

3.7

'The fundamental psychological law ... is that men are disposed as a rule to increase their consumption as their income increases but not by as much as their income increases.'

Source: J.M. Keynes The General Theory of Employment Interest and Money Macmillan London 1936

3.9

Source: Kingston Finance

3.8

A fast road to heartbreak

A FAST loan seemed the perfect answer to all the financial problems of Terry and Carole Smith. But it lead to thoughts of suicide.

The Smiths had just returned from holiday, short of cash, and wondered how they could pay for Christmas. Then Terry saw an advert offering no-delay finance, and when he asked for a loan Terry was told the County Court debt judgment against him didn't matter.

The couple's home was signed over as security for £4,850. Repayments with 39 per cent interest a year would add up to more than £17,000. Plus their broker had to be paid £850.

Paying the huge sum became impossible. The marriage went on the rocks, and the couple's two children couldn't understand why Carole was always in tears.

Carole, 35, from Birkenhead, Merseyside, recalls: "It couldn't have been easier to get money. But when we knew we couldn't afford the payments we realised we could lose our home.

"It destroyed us. I think I would have rather put a shotgun to my head. I was having nightmares."

Source: The Sunday Mirror August 9 1987

ACTIVITY 2

Two other concepts are used when analysing the relationship between income and consumption – the marginal propensity to consume (MPC) and the average propensity to consume (APC).

A Using the figures in data 3.6 calculate the APC and MPC for each level of income. Use data 3.10 to help you.

B What happens to the APC and the MPC when income rises?

C Using the figures in data 3.11 attempt questions A and B above again. Are your conclusions the same?

3.10

$$APC = \frac{Total\ Consumption}{Total\ Income}$$

This illustrates how much is spent from total income

eg $\frac{7400}{8000} = 0.925$

$$MPC = \frac{Change\ in\ Consumption}{Change\ in\ Income}$$

This illustrates how much is spent out of any increase in income

eg $\frac{8200-7400}{9000-8000} = \frac{800}{1000} = 0.8$ or 80 per cent

3.11

Personal disposable income £ million	Consumer expenditure £ million
53,803	48,510
54,676	48,703
55,576	48,894

ACTIVITY 3

Examine Article 3.12.

A What is the difference between permanent and disposable income?

B How will the permanent income consumption function differ from the Keynesian consumption function?

3.12
Permanent-income Hypothesis

In recent years a rather different view of the consumption function has been developed. Basically, the permanent-income hypothesis holds that consumption doesn't depend on *current* disposable income but rather on some measure of expected, or long term permanent, income. The planning period may be anywhere from two to five years, or even longer, depending upon people's expectations. According to this theory in the short-run, consumption will not drop drastically even if, for some reason, people's income falls below what they think their permenant income is. Conversely, consumption will not increase very much even if people's income suddenly jumps above the level they consider to be permanent. The permanent income hypothesis suggests that the propensity to consume (APC/MPC) may vary in the short run, but will be stable in the long run. Friedman argues that the APC will not fall; a high income earner is just as likely to spend all income, in the long run, as a low income earner. In the UK, the APC and MPC are approximately 0.9.

Source: Adapted in part from *Economics Explained* P. Maunder, D. Myres, N. Wall, Roger LeRoy Miller Collins Education London 1987

ACTIVITY 4

Classical economists argued that the rate of interest was a key factor in determining the level of savings. Interest was the reward to a person for parting with their purchasing power, so higher interest rates were an incentive to spend less and save more (and vice versa).

Keynes however, argued that consumption was the stronger motive and that people spend in relation to their income and save what they could afford. Banks and building societies thus compete with each other through interest rates and effectively compete savings from each other rather than attracting extra savings from the public.

A Examine data 3.14 and calculate the APS for each of the years from 1979 to 1985. Use data 3.13 to help you.

B Examine data 3.14 and 3.15. Is there any accurate relationship between the level of interest rates and the percentage of income saved?

Any income not spent on consumption is saved – therefore it is possible from the data to plot a savings function. This will be the complement of the consumption function in data 3.5.

C Examine data 3.16. What is happening between points A and B? What is the relationship between data 3.5 showing the consumption function and data 3.16 showing the savings function?

3.13

$$APS = \frac{Total\ Savings}{Total\ Income}$$

$$MPS = \frac{Change\ in\ Savings}{Change\ in\ Income}$$

3.14

How much do we save?

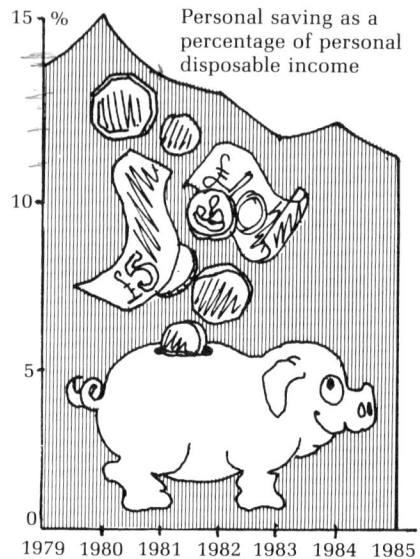

Personal saving as a percentage of personal disposable income

Source: Adapted from *New Society* April 1987

3.15

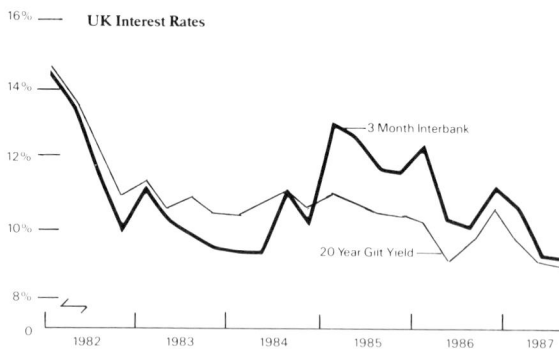

UK Interest Rates

3 Month Interbank

20 Year Gilt Yield

Source: *Barclays Review* August 1987

3.16

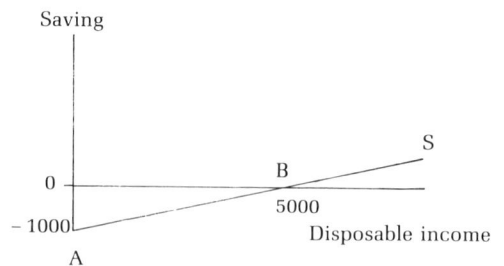

Saving

Disposable income

TASK 3 To examine the determinants of investment in an economy.

Investment is the creation of capital equipment for use in the production process. As such it is a demand for a firm's output from other firms and so helps to generate output and increase national income. However, it can either be new investment or merely replace old, worn out equipment (depreciation). Any investment project will require detailed financial analysis before a decision can be reached to proceed, even if the funds do not have to be borrowed but are made available either through undistributed profits or fresh share capital (because there is an opportunity cost involved).

ACTIVITY 1
Using items 3.17–3.20 answer the following questions:

A Is investment directly influenced by income?

B What do you think is meant by 'the projected rate of return is (only) around ten per cent'?

C What is the maximum rate of interest that would be appropriate to make such an investment project profitable?

D If interest rates were to increase what might happen to the viability of the project? Is it likely the project would be abandoned
● if it was just starting?
● if it was half completed?

E How would BR evaluate if a new line could be justified financially?

F What role do estimates of passenger/freight traffic play in evaluating the rate of return? How will the degree of optimism or pessimism in these estimates affect the viability of the project?

G What opportunities would BR be missing if they failed to convert any lines to the continental loading gauge? How might environmental benefit be taken into account?

H What effect would statements like those in 3.19 have on investment in the project?

3.17
An Investment Demand Schedule

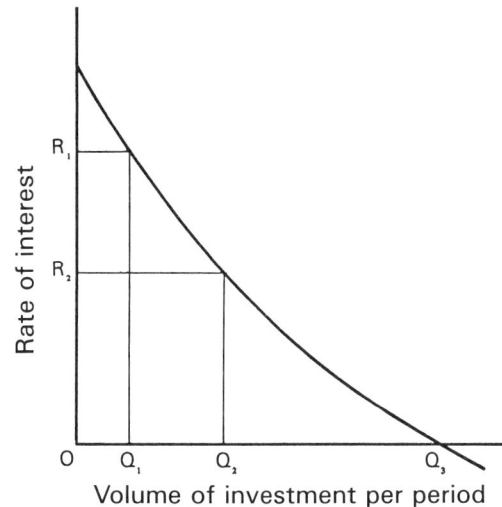

3.18

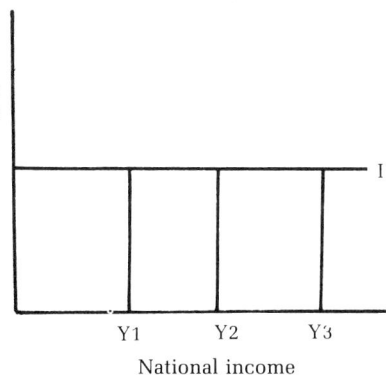

3.19
'The only remaining obstacle to the building of the channel tunnel is the share flotation. The free travel offers for the new tunnel makes this issue an excellent buy for long-term investors.'

'The viability of the tunnel project has been based on overestimates of potential traffic flows. Investment in the project involves a higher risk than previous flotations.'

Source: The Guardian August 28 1987

3.20

The 186 mph Train a Grande Vitesse (TGV): it will reach speeds of only 60 mph on the British stretch of the continental run on a track with standards well below other main lines from London

BR'S SLOW TRAIN TO PARIS

With the agreement of £5 billion worth of bank loans only one major obstacle now remains in the way of Eurotunnel's £750 million flotation this October. Before the prospectus can be released the French and Belgian governments must agree a formula to link the public and private finance for the new lines to carry the 186mph TGV trains from Calais to Paris and Brussels. A third of the French investment of £1.8 billion is for a fleet of 64 TGV's (out of a total fleet of 100) to link London, Paris, Brussels, and Cologne. Both governments however want the whole TGV project to be financed privately.

However while the projected rate of return on the project is only around 10 per cent some guarantees will be necessary – and the revenue forecasts in the prospectus assume that 16 million rail passengers will use the tunnel in its first operational year – 1993.

The major problem for the French part of the operation is BR's reticence in upgrading British lines to increase speed or capacity. BR is committed to a 'leave alone' policy since the ever increasing cost of a new Dover–London route was largely responsible for the cancellation of the last tunnel project in 1975. The French however cannot understand the logic when Nicholas Ridley (then Transport Secretary) claims the M20 extension from Maidstone to Ashford is environmentally acceptable while an upgraded railway line is environmentally damaging. However the French are worried that any attempt to force BR to increase the basic £400 million investment could kill the project. Moreover Mrs Thatcher is worried that if BR did increase this investment she could be accused of pouring more public money into the project via the back door.

BR Chairman, Sir Robert Reid, does not however believe the new line can be justified financially. Half of the £400 million is for new rolling stock and only £20 million is for improved track and signalling on the main Eurotunnel route. Thus TGV's will only average 60 mph on the British Section compared to 100 mph on the newly electrified East Coast main line. If the East Coast is electrified why not the South Coast?

A very basic improvement package should at least be possible – for example upgrading the straight Tonbridge-Tunnel section to 140 mph (though this would require overhead power) would increase speed, while upgrading the Orpington-Tunnel section from two track to four track would significantly increase line capacity. BR is currently evaluating the financial case for this based on higher traffic estimates.

BR's biggest mistake however is in missing out on a potential freight bonanza if they fail to convert any routes to the Continental loading gauge (UK trains are a foot lower and narrower than continental trains so our bridges and tunnels are smaller). Estimates suggest conversion could increase freight traffic four fold and have the environmental benefit of reducing M25 traffic by up to a quarter. However it would require the development of a fleet of wagons that fit the BR loading gauge, carrying road trailers 'piggy back' on wagons or putting rail wheels under road trailers. Standard road trailers will not go under BR bridges and BR has rejected the conversion of even one route from the Midlands to the Continent as too expensive. This is naive because the bulk of the conversion cost is not, as first thought in moving the tracks apart because road trailers are narrower than BR wagons, but in obtaining an extra foot in height. BR may regret neglecting this investment opportunity.

Therefore, while the new TGV lines on the Continent might realise their full potential, Britain may lose both financial and environmental benefits through its shortsighted failure to match the levels of investment on the Continent.

Source: Adapted from an article by Richard Hope *The Guardian* August 28 1987

ACTIVITY 2
Read items 3.21 and 3.22 and answer the following questions.

A Will a company need to make replacement or new investment if it has:
  • falling sales?
  • stable sales?
  • increasing sales?

B How will a prudent company try to finance replacement investment?

C If the ratio of capital: output is 5:1 what effect will an increase in demand of £100 million have on new investment demand if:
  • increased demand is expected to be temporary?
  • increased demand is expected to be permanent?

D If consumer demand stopped rising what effect would this have on the level of new investment? What effect would this have on aggregate demand?

3.21

Capital equipment deteriorates with use or may indeed become obsolete. This is known as capital consumption or depreciation. Therefore some investment will be necessary just to replace old worn out equipment.

3.22

The investment in any piece of machinery will probably cost more than its annual value of output, but because it has a long life its returns will make it viable. Therefore a modest increase in national income and consumer demand can generate a much greater increase in Investment and thus a further massive increase in aggregate demand. This is known as the 'Accelerator Theory' and goes a long way towards explaining the rapid nature of economic recoveries.

TASK 4 To discover the nature of equilibrium in a simple economy.

The public receive incomes for their part in the production process, and they spend part of this income on buying consumption goods from firms. Thus there is a **circular flow of income**. However not all income returns directly to firms – that which is saved is withdrawn and does not create a demand for goods, though it is available for use in financial institutions. Not all demand for goods and services however comes from the public – firms invest in capital equipment so this is an injection of demand into the circular flow. For equilibrium to exist all output must be sold without any shortage or excess of demand. Producers will therefore have no plans to cut or increase output. For this to be the case all incomes paid to the public must return as aggregate demand in purchasing the output produced and any savings withdrawn must be exactly replaced by the investment injected. Savings will provide the main source of funds for investment but as the two decisions are taken by different sets of people there is no necessity for them to be equal. The equilibrium position is explained in data 3.23–3.25.

3.23

Equilibrium national income is where there is no pressure for change – income and output will remain the same in each time period.

3.25

Equilibrium is where

FUTURE INCOME	= CONSUMPTION	+ INVESTMENT
(Y)	= (C)	+ (I)

or alternatively

PLANNED SAVINGS	= PLANNED INVESTMENT
(S)	= (I)
ie WITHDRAWALS	= INJECTIONS

3.24

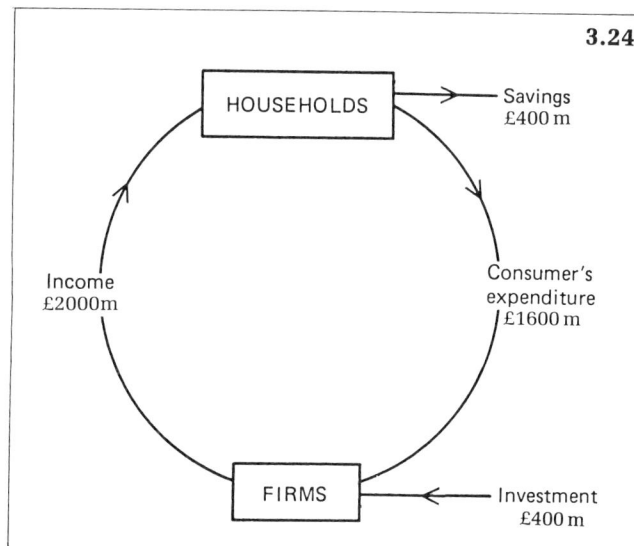

ACTIVITY 1

The economy does not always have to be in equilibrium; if investment is greater than savings then income will rise; if saving is greater than investment income will fall as aggregate demand is less than output.

Examine Table 3.26

A In which week is the economy in equilibrium?

B In this week prove that Y = C + I and S = I.

C Why is the economy not in equilibrium in the other weeks?

			3.26

WEEKS

	1	2	3	4 ....n
1 Output (= income)	100	90	82	75·6	50
2 Investment	10	10	10	10	10
3 Planned saving (20% of Row 1)		20	18	16·4	15·1	10
4 Consumption goods demanded (80%) of Row 1)		80	72	65·6	60·5	40

Source: Adapted from *An Introduction to National Income Analysis* W. Beckerman Weidenfeld and Nicolson London 1968

TASK 5   To analyse which factors determine the levels of aggregate demand, output and national income in a full economy.

A full economy is one which includes a government sector and foreign trade as well as consumption investment and savings. The government raises money by taxing income earners and spends this money on a variety of activities including education, health and defence. The UK's trade is reflected in the balance of payments which is an account of trade in goods, services and finance with the rest of the world. Imports take money out of the country while exports earn money.

ACTIVITY 1

A Using the definitions in 3.28 classify the following into withdrawals or injections:
EXPORTS
IMPORTS
TAXATION
GOVERNMENT EXPENDITURE

B What effect will each of the four items in 3.29 have on national income?

C Write down 2 formulae for equilibrium in an open economy (you may wish to refer to data 3.30 and 3.25 to help you).

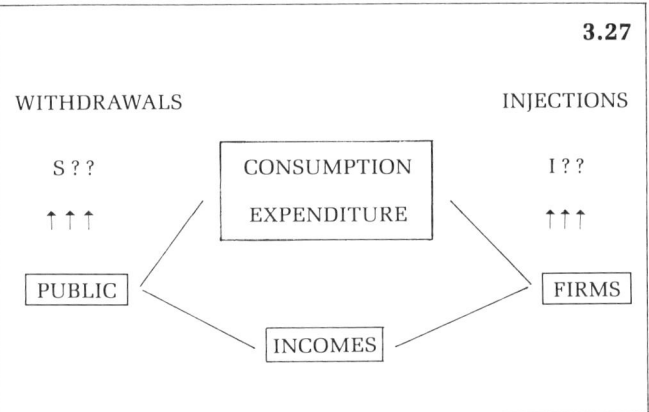

3.27

3.28
Withdrawals are that part of the public's income which does not directly return to British firms in the purchase of goods and services and which therefore tend to reduce the size of aggregate demand and, in consequence, national income.
Injections are elements of expenditure on goods and services which do not come from the British public – they therefore tend to increase the size of aggregate demand and national income.

3.29
BUDGET SURPLUS: Taxation > Government Expenditure
BUDGET DEFICIT: Taxation < Government Expenditure
BALANCE OF PAYMENTS SURPLUS: Exports > Imports
BALANCE OF PAYMENTS DEFICIT: Exports < Imports

ACTIVITY 2

You should now be able to work out and draw on the diagram the effects of an increase or a decrease in aggregate demand. This is indicated by a shift of the AD line to the left or the right as indicated in data 3.30 and 3.36. However any change in aggregate demand will have a much greater effect on national income than this initial change, and this relationship is known as the multiplier.

Read Article 3.32.

A What effect is the complex likely to have on the local economy?

B In what ways might this extend beyond the initial cost of the complex?

3.30

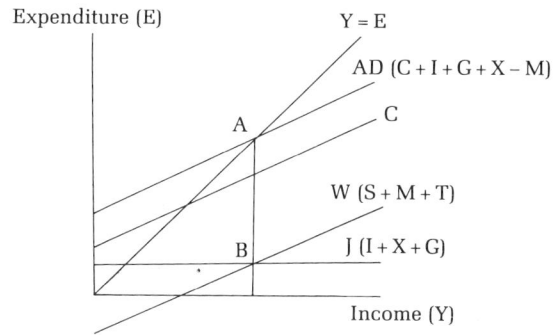

Equilibrium can now be shown on a diagram. All injections into the economy are autonomous (independent of national income and affected by other factors) and so are horizontal. Equilibrium therefore can be demonstrated in two ways:

(1) OUTPUT = AGGREGATE DEMAND
Y = Consumption + investment + government + (exports − imports)

(2) WITHDRAWALS = INJECTIONS
W = J
Savings + imports + taxation = Investment + exports + government spending.

3.31

The **multiplier** is the name given to the process whereby an initial change in aggregate spending in the economy leads to a much larger eventual or ultimate change in aggregate spending.

3.32

Plan for huge retail centre unveiled

By Barbara Metcalfe

A MAJOR new initiative costing £80 million and creating 1,500 new jobs was unveiled in Southport today.

The proposal by London and Manchester-based developers Sibec was announced at a press conference hosted by Sefton Borough Council.

But planning permission is still to be given to the scheme, which would cover 10 acres of land and provide a "unique high street theatre experience."

The proposal will go before the council next month. If granted, work would start early next year.

Sibec chief executive Mike Birchall said the development would reflect the historic themes of previous buildings on the site — the Winter Gardens and the Lord Street railway station.

He said the 600,000 sq. ft. complex will include modern shop units arranged around a naturally lit glazed mall space with restaurants, food courts and halls, a children's world and other family attractions.

There would be provision for a major department store, several medium sized stores and 80 smaller shop units.

Victorian

There would be car parking for 1,000 vehicles and 250 staff cars.

The intention, he said, was to retain the Victorian frontage of the building, which has been used recently as the bus station on Lord Street.

A new 150 bedroom hotel would be a prominent feature of the scheme, designed in a crescent form above the shopping centre and overlooking the seafront.

Expand

He said: "The development would transform Southport into one of the most important retail locations in the North West, attracting shoppers and visitors from a wide area.

"Sibec expects the hotel to expand the town's tourist trade and, together with establishing Southport as an important business location, will provide a significant long-term boost for the local economy."

He said they anticipated the £40 million building contract would commence in mid-1988 with the two-level shopping and leisure galleries of the new Winter Gardens in 1991.

He said: "It will quickly establish itself as the most unique and exciting centre in Western Europe."

£80m SEASIDE SPECTACULAR!

A model of the new complex showing the new crescent-shaped hotel in the foreground

Source: *The Liverpool Echo* September 4 1987

ACTIVITY 3

Examine data 3.33 and 3.34.

A Calculate the value of the multiplier (K) when the marginal propensity to consume (mpc) is:

0.9
0.8
0.75
0.6
0.4
0.25

Use data 3.33 and 3.34 to help you.

3.33

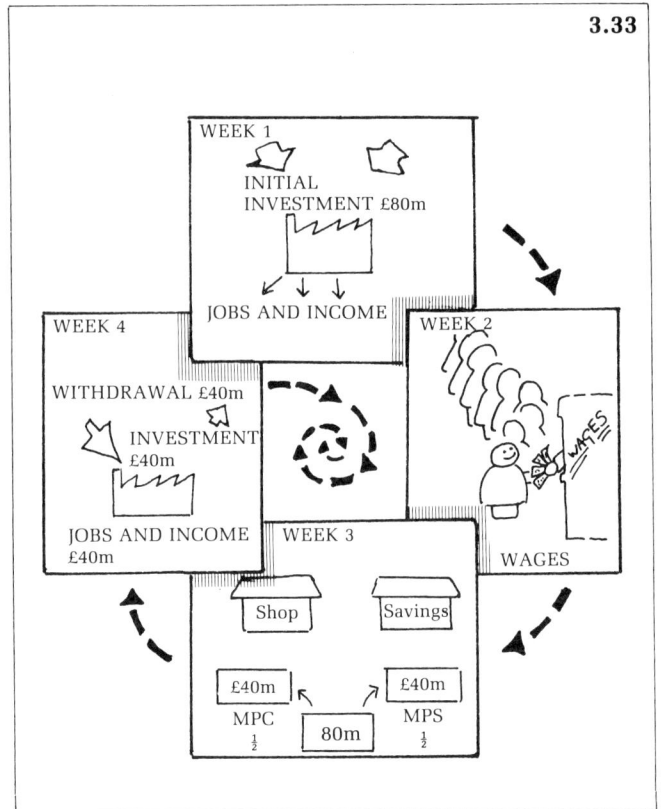

3.34

Example: Initial Investment = £80 million

The multiplier shows how an initial change in demand (in this case investment) leads to a much greater increase in income. The part of this increased income which goes on consumption (in this case assume MPC = 0.5) further increases income while that part which is withdrawn (which must therefore also equal 0.5) does not.

Therefore the increases in income is:
£80m + £40m + £20m + £10m + ...

Final change in income:
$\Delta Y = K \Delta$ demand $\Delta Y = £80$ million $\times K$.

K can be calculated easily by using the formula:

$$K = \frac{1}{1 - MPC} = \frac{1}{0.5} = 2$$

Therefore the final increase in income:
£80 million $\times$ 2 = £160 million.

ACTIVITY 4

In an open economy there is more than one withdrawal. There are three methods which remove the public's income that could be potentially spent on British goods – savings, taxation and imports.

A Using data 3.35, calculate the final increase in income.

B If income was £2000 million before the initial change in injections what is the final income figure?

C What similarities are there between the multiplier and the accelerator theory of investment?

3.35

Marginal propensity to consume	= 0.5 (MPC)
Marginal propensity to save	= 0.2 (MPS)
Marginal propensity to import	= 0.1 (MPM)
Marginal propensity to be taxed	= 0.2 (MPT)

Initial change in demand (injections)

Government expenditure	+ £100million
Investment	+ £200million

$$K = \frac{1}{MPS + MPM + MPT} \text{ or } \frac{1}{1 - MPC}$$

ACTIVITY 5

Keynes argued that, when the situation warranted it, it was the role of the government to increase aggregate demand to expand the economy by using fiscal and monetary policies.

A   What methods of fiscal and monetary policy are suggested in articles 3.37 and 3.38 which could bring about the shift indicated in diagram 3.36?

B   What potential problems and benefits of increasing aggregate demand are suggested in articles 3.37 and 3.38?

3.36

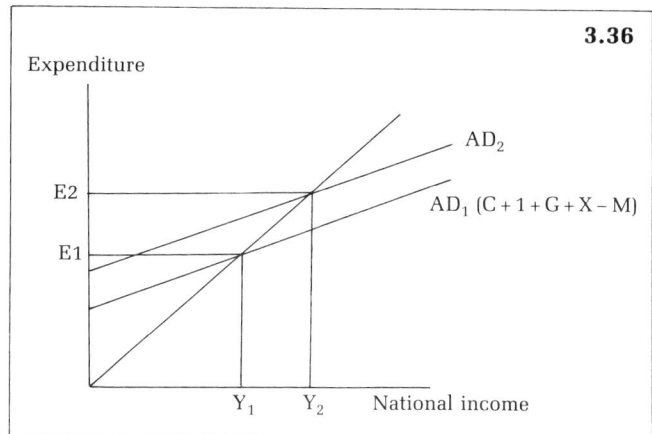

Expenditure / National income diagram showing AD_2 and $AD_1 (C + 1 + G + X - M)$, with E_2, E_1 on the Expenditure axis and Y_1, Y_2 on the National income axis.

3.37

The boom turns into huge slump

City experts predict a cash crisis, runaway inflation and spiralling taxation if Labour get the chance to run—and ruin—our economy.

Britain is booming after eight years of Tory leadership. Inflation is down from double figures in 1979 to less than four per cent. The pound is strong and business leaders report bulging order books.

On the jobless front, dole queues have dropped non-stop for the past seven months and will soon dip below the crucial three million barrier. All that will change if Mr Kinnock and his "spend, spend, spend" cronies take over.

The last Labour government of 1974–79 brought runaway inflation, rising unemployment and a slump in industry.

High taxation and borrowing was necessary to fund big public spending programmes.

And Professor Patrick Minford of Liverpool University, says it could all happen again if Labour get in on Thursday. He predicts:
■ A massive slump in production.
■ A very weak pound which would hit British holidaymakers abroad.
■ Inflation racing above ten per cent.

Professor Minford does not pull his punches.

Looking at the Tory record he says "Mrs Thatcher's policies have not been universally successful in rolling back Britain's problems.

Inflation has been brought down, productivity is up, growth is good and tax rates have come down."

Crisis

"But unemployment has risen to more than three million and has only recently started to fall."

With the same hard-hitting approach, he warns darkly against the dangers of Labour's plans.

He says: "By universal agreement, Labour's policies would increase inflation sharply.

This would raise interest rates and cause a sterling crisis.

At best, the prospects for output and unemployment under Labour offer a temporary boost.

At worst, they offer a permanent decline."

Professor Minford says Labour's battle to bring down the dole queues would be lost and output would also suffer.

Rising inflation and interest rates fuelled by Labour's higher taxes and increased public spending would scare off investors.

And that would mean spending on factories and investment in British Industry would fall as money-men started looking abroad for a safer bet.

Professor Minford sums up: "To sacrifice the control of inflation for such an uncertain prospect seems an indefensible policy."

Source: *The Sun* June 8 1987

INFLATION ADJUSTED KEYNESIANS... AND TAX CUTS

Usually the Conservative Party conference is accompanied by a small but strategic cut in interest rates. The fact that this has not happened this year should not hide the Chancellor's keenness to cut interest rates to stimulate the economy. The real question however is how effective are interest rate cuts in stimulating the economy – Switzerland has had low interest rates but slow growth whereas America's high interest rates have been accompanied by fast growth. America's investment is booming despite the high interest rates. Such facts tend to prove the Chancellor wrong.

There is today considerable economic research which stresses the effectiveness of budgetary policy showing that tax and government expenditure changes do affect real output and jobs. Research has shown a considerable correlation between a new concept – the 'real budget deficit' and output growth and jobs. The crude budget figures are not regarded as a good indicator of government policy because they are affected by many other influences besides the policy itself, particularly the trade cycle and inflation. A slump automatically reduces tax revenue and increases benefit spending thus creating a deficit without any policy decision having been taken. Inflation also reduces the value of real government debt. The 'real budget' figure therefore eliminates the effects of the trade cycle and inflation on the budget and has come up with some startling correlations with output and jobs.

While most practical people have always accepted that tax cuts stimulate the economy, monetarists contend that the resultant deficit financing will raise interest rates, crowding out the effects of the tax cuts.

The 'real budget' however is a new analytical tool by which 'inflation adjusted Keynesians' can reinterpret the importance of fiscal policy on output and jobs.

Nevertheless there are drawbacks in this new analysis – calculating the budget figures adjusted for the cycle and inflation requires some assumptions about the rate of growth of the economy required to maintain full employment. Moreover there can also be changes on the supply side such as productivity increases (which cut costs and prices and increase real demand). Such price cuts reduce the real value of government debt and thus the real government deficit.

Thus instead of the real budget deficit spurring growth the increased output increases the real deficit – 'the cause' becomes the 'effect'.

This apparent link between real deficits and jobs is not supposed to imply that in each and every case fiscal policy can be used to expand an economy. Tax cuts or spending increases implemented when the economy is near full employment are likely to cause a rise in inflation (due to rising import prices as the exchange rate falls, or higher wage demands and therefore costs) which will negate the effects of the tax cuts. This may be the stage that the budget-fed American economy is about to reach.

Nevertheless the 'real budget' is a useful analytical addition which reasserts the importance of fiscal policy. The American deficit hasn't just forced up interest rates but has also created the current boom.

Perhaps this is why Nigel Lawson is for tax cuts after all.

Source: Adapted from *The Guardian* 1985

SECTION 4 Unemployment

HYPOTHESIS	Unemployment can only be reduced by a balanced approach acting on both the demand and the supply side of the economy.

Full employment was one of the stated economic policy aims of successive governments from 1945 to 1979. By 'full employment' politicians meant an unemployment total of below 500,000 people, out of a work-force of approximately 25 million. Before 1971, unemployment had never risen above 3 per cent of the working population. Since then however, unemployment has increased dramatically, topping 13½ per cent, or 3¼ million in 1985. Data 4.1 and 4.2 indicate conflicting views about present and future unemployment trends.

4.1

'Mass unemployment in UK "here to stay".'

Source: *The Guardian* September 1987

4.2

'Jobless cut by 118,111 as wages race ahead.'

Source: *Today* November 13 1987

TASK 1 To discover why unemployment is considered to be a problem.

ACTIVITY 1
Examine data 4.3

A Describe the predicted changes in occupational employment from 1986–1995.

B Why is it expected that part-time work will increase disproportionately to full-time work?

C Which groups in society are likely to gain most and lose most by the changes described?

D Are you optimistic or pessimistic about unemployment in the near future and the next ten years? State your reasons.

4.3

2.5m still on dole queue by 1995, report predicts

Mass unemployment in UK 'here to stay'

By Christopher Huhne,
Economics Editor

The growth of the economy is likely to continue to be on a par with the fast growth before the first oil crisis in 1973. But the resulting stimulus to jobs is only enough to bring unemployment down gradually to 2.8 million by 1990 and 2.5 million by the end of 1995.

Women part-timers will benefit most from the growth of job opportunities.

These are some of the conclusions of the annual review of the economy and employment published yesterday by the University of Warwick's Institute for Employment Research, one of the leading publicly supported centres into the research of job structure and medium term prospects.

Overall, employment is expected to increase at about 0.5 per cent a year, with the growth going disproportionately to part-timers as it has done recently, mainly as a result of the nature of the fastest growing employment sectors in the service industries.

Part-timers were 21 per cent of all employees in 1981; 23.3 per cent in 1986 and are projected to rise to 28 per cent by 1995.

Because five out of six part-time jobs go to women, the number of female employees is expected to increase by a million until women form almost half of all employees – 48 per cent against their present 45 per cent share. This growth is mainly in business and miscellaneous services and health, education and public administration.

The fortunes of the main economic sectors are expected to differ substantially. Jobs will fall by 1 per cent a year over the period until 1995 in the primary and utilities sector (including North Sea oil, gas, and mining). Manufacturing also continues to lose jobs, although again at a slower rate than the 3 per cent a year since 1975.

The decline is expected to be 1 per cent a year, or a total of 500,000 jobs.

The job gains come in construction (plus 170,000); distribution and transport (plus 340,000) mainly in hotels and catering; business and miscellaneous services (plus 1.4 million); and non-marketed services such as health and education (plus 100,000). Business services jobs grow at 3 per cent a year, compared with 3.75 per cent a year between 1975 and 1986, mainly because of slightly higher productivity growth.

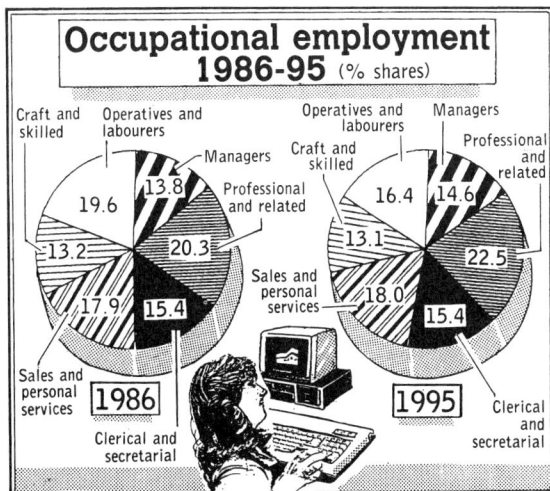

Occupational employment 1986-95 (% shares)

1986:
- Craft and skilled 19.6
- Operatives and labourers 13.8
- Managers 13.2
- Professional and related 20.3
- Sales and personal services 17.9
- Clerical and secretarial 15.4

1995:
- Operatives and labourers 16.4
- Managers 14.6
- Professional and related 22.5
- Craft and skilled 13.1
- Sales and personal services 18.0
- Clerical and secretarial 15.4

Source: *The Guardian* September 1987

ACTIVITY 2
In data 4.4 John McIlroy describes the costs of unemployment. Considering the money costs of job creation outlined in data 4.5, explain whether you think unemployment is a cheap or an expensive problem.

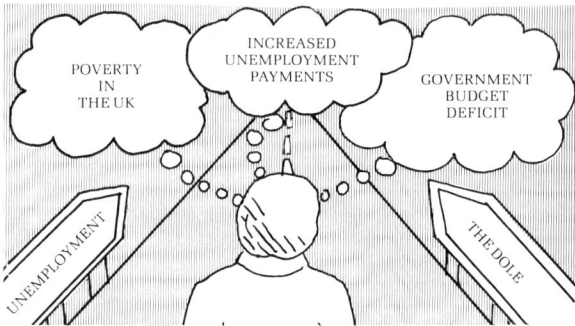

Source: Adapted from 'Unemployment and the economy' John McIlroy from *Political Issues in Britain Today* B Jones Manchester University Press 1985

4.4

The impact of unemployment

(1) **Cost to the state**
This includes the cost of unemployment pay, supplementary benefit and redundancy payments as well as a loss of income tax, National Insurance, VAT and other taxes on spending. In 1980 it was estimated that tax losses and benefit payments represented £4,128 million in lost public spending. In 1983 Labour argued before the election, that unemployment figures represented a loss of £17 billion in tax, which rose to a cost of £30 billion when added to lost production and benefit payments.

(2) **Cost to the individual**
Even though we have a Welfare State those on long-term supplementary benefit may well live in officially defined poverty. In 1979 Townsend found workers who had been out of work for ten weeks or more were two and a half times more likely to live in poverty than those who had not been unemployed. Recent studies by the DES have shown that over 50 per cent of 2,000 unemployed men surveyed had state benefits of less than half their previous earnings.

(3) **The social cost**
Studies have shown a strong relationship between unemployment and social problems. A 1984 report by Professor John Cox showed death rates to be 21 per cent higher than expected in unemployed men. They were also twice as likely to have committed suicide and 80 per cent more likely to have a fatal accident.

(4) **The inequality cost**
The poorest suffer most from unemployment, particularly the unskilled, young, women and coloured workers. It also creates divisions between regions and communities as illustrated in the 1984 miners' strike.

4.5
The net cost, after taking into account the sums flowing back to the government, in tax and National Insurance contributions of one YTS place is £1,200 and one place on the Community Programme costs £1,800. The gross cost of one extra local government job is £8,000 and one extra construction job costs £4,000.

Source: Adapted from the *Daily Telegraph* January 30 1985

ACTIVITY 3
Unemployment has sometimes been likened to 'enforced leisure time'. Consider data 4.6 and 4.7. Do you agree or disagree with this? Explain your answer.

ACTIVITY 4
Using all the data in this task, write an essay entitled 'Unemployment: the economic and social evil of our time'.

4.6
The world of the future holds many surprises. The thing that occupies most of the people for most of the time – work – will become a thing of the past. Machines will make the worker redundant. How will they cope? Left with endless hours of idleness, those who cannot cope may destroy themselves and their world. People are bored without something to do. What of this brave new world? It is already happening, mostly in cities. Only the educated and innovative will survive. The rest will make do with the boredom of TV re-runs as long as they can.

Source: Adapted from *New Society* November 29 1979

4.7

Jobless in Wolverhampton

TASK 2   To discover how unemployment is measured.

The Department of Employment defines the working population as 'persons over sixteen who work for pay or gain, or who register themselves as "actively seeking" work and meanwhile claiming benefit'. To be an unemployment statistic, therefore, one must be registered as a claimant at an unemployment benefit office, but not all those who would class themselves as seeking work are entitled to claim benefit. For example, all men over 60 no longer have to sign on to claim benefit; school leavers who leave after their exams are not entitled to claim benefit until the September of their school leaving year. Thus the official statistics contain some hidden unemployment. There is considerable political debate over precisely how many people are actually unemployed. Commentators from the 'Left' and 'Right' would criticise the official total as either under or over-estimating the total numbers out of work.

ACTIVITY 1
Data 4.8 outlines the controversy. Using the October 1983 total as a starting point, decide which of the additions/subtractions you agree with. Explain your choices.

4.8

JOBLESS – THE GREAT DIVIDE
Official total: 3,094,000

Left-wing critics ADD:

Unemployed excluded by statistical changes, October 1982 (net)	189,000
Unemployed over-sixties (no longer required to register)[1]	199,000
Short-time working	43,000
Students on vacation	27,000
Effect of Special Employment Measures	395,000
Unregistered unemployed[2]	490,000
Total additions	**1,343,000**
TOTAL UNEMPLOYED	**4,437,000**

1. Of whom 37,000 were removed between December 1981 and February 1982 and a further 162,000 as a result of Budget 1983 measures.
2. Estimate based on Dept of Employment survey, 1981.

Right-wing critics SUBTRACT:

School leavers	168,000
Claimants who are not really looking for jobs[1]	490,000
Severely disabled	23,000
'Unemployables' – mentally or physically incapable[2]	135,000
'Job changers' – out of work for four weeks or less	360,000
'Black economy' workers, illegally claiming benefit[3]	250,000
Total subtractions	**1,426,000**
TOTAL UNEMPLOYED	**1,668,000**

1. Estimate, based on 1981 Labour Force Survey.
2. Dept of Employment estimate.
3. Unknowable: estimate based on internal government survey suggesting 8% of claims not justified.

Source: *The Sunday Times* November 6 1983

ACTIVITY 2
It is important to appreciate that the official total of unemployed people does not represent a stagnant pool of labour; on the contrary, there are inflows and outflows and it is therefore very important to consider the statistics by examining the length of time people are unemployed. Look at data 4.9. Describe the April 1987 unemployment pattern by duration and how it changed during the year since April 1986.

4.9

Unemployment by duration–April 1987

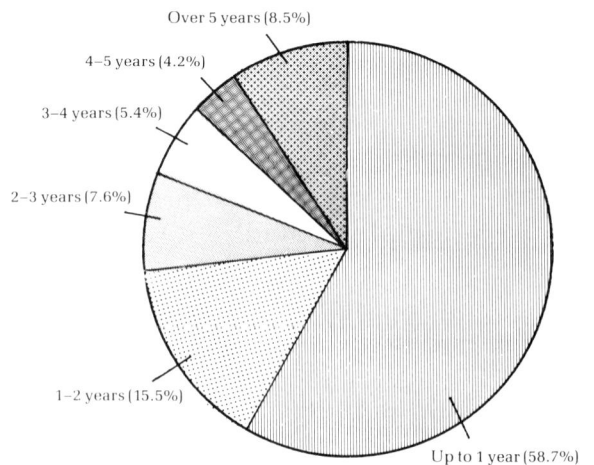

Change since April 1986 (GB thousands)

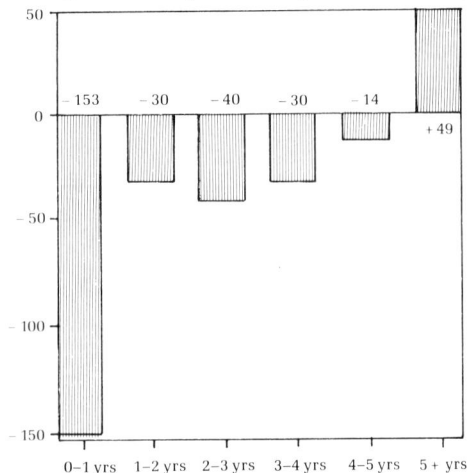

Source: Department of Employment

ACTIVITY 3

Consider data 4.10. To obtain an accurate picture of the nature of the unemployment problem it is important to examine more than just raw unemployment data.

A   Describe the changes in educational and economic activity of 16 year olds in England from 1975–85.

B   Do you agree with the author when he says there is '. . . a sizeable ghost army of un-employed 16–18 year olds . . .'?

C   What other ghost armies might there be amongst other groups in society?

4.10

Jobless figures ignore 50,000

The existence of a sizeable ghost army of unemployed 16 to 18-year-olds who do not appear in the official figures has been confirmed by the Department of Education and Science.

The Department estimates that around 50,000 youngsters are ignored in the unemployment count because they are not on the dole. Soon after the last general election the government changed the rules, so that people are only registered as unemployed if they successfully claim benefit.

The DES reckons that another 70,000 in the same age group have left education but, for one reason or another, are not seeking work. Around half of these are 18-year-old girls (who may have simply been discouraged from entering the labour market by current conditions).

The estimates are made in an analysis of the educational and economic activity of 16 to 18-year-olds produced by the DES in collaboration with the Department of Employment and the Man-power Services Commission. It shows that the proportion of the age-group who are 'in employment' fell from 72 per cent in 1975 to 45 per cent last year, and that most of the drop was between 1980 and 1984.

The DES is careful to place inverted commas around the term 'in employment' because, while the figures do not include those in the Youth Training Scheme, they do count in as employed – because of the way the statistics are obtained – the estimated 120,000 non-working youngsters referred to above.

The DES says that the change has been most marked among 16-year-olds, of whom fewer than two in ten were 'in employment' in January of last year, compared with more than six out of ten in 1975.

Source: *The Times Educational Supplement* June 5 1987

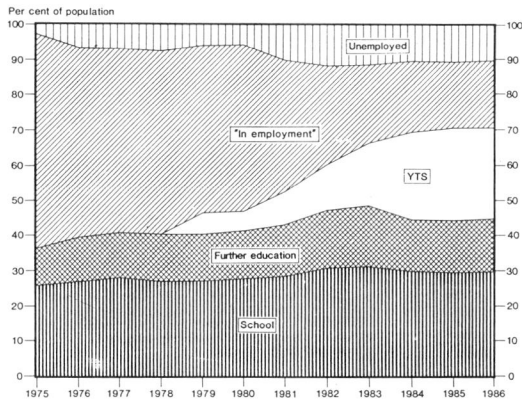

Educational and economic activity of 16 year olds in England

ACTIVITY 4

Equally, there are those on the register who are not entitled to unemployment benefits under current regulations. Read the extract in data 4.11. How might the Department of Employment's activities destroy the incentive to work?

4.11

Fiddlers on the Dole

The return the Department of Employment has achieved since it stepped up its fraud investigations—Merseyside had just five full-time investigators a few years ago, but now has 26—has been steady and, in its potential for helping squeeze the number of registered unemployed below the psychological three million mark in time for an early election, dramatic.

In the nine months to the end of last year, 710 investigators nation-wide looked at 260,000 claims. The result was that 41,000 were with-drawn, and there were 2,565 prosecutions. The Department estimate is that this saved a net figure of £29.3 million in unemployment benefit.

But it admits it is uncertain how long the average claimant then remains 'off the books'. As John Stansfield put it: 'If I get him off now because he's working, and that job ends, he is quite entitled to come back on again. But I might just give him the incentive he needs to make something of what he is doing already.'

'It is sometimes easier to see them as likeable rogues than as criminals. But the people we find tend to get bills from the Inland Revenue soon afterwards. The same people are not paying their National Insurance contributions, not paying their VAT or income tax, and they've often got the police looking for them as well.'

Source: The *Sunday Telegraph* March 29 1987

TASK 3   To discover the main types of unemployment.

Having discovered that the unemployment total does not represent an unchanging pool of people, but that it does represent a 'snap shot' of a flow of people to and from the unemployment register, you need to identify the reasons why these people are out of work at a particular time. This is important, as we shall see later, since if we are to consider policy solutions to unemployment, we must break down the global figure into its constituent parts. Economists usually classify unemployment under one of four headings.

ACTIVITY 1
Study data 4.12. Using the headlines as a guide, write a definition for each type of unemployment.

4.12

CROSS CHEQUES?
Cashiers at Natmidlays Kings Cross branch are angry as the bank unveiled plans to install more automatic cash dispeners next year

STRUCTURAL

WANTED: FRUIT PICKERS
Sept–Oct only

Contact: M Scroggins
Fruity Farm
Nr Barnworth

SEASONAL

JOB CHANGERS SIGN ON

'Scandalous' say MPs

FRICTIONAL

WORLD SLUMP HITS UK MANUFACTURING ! EXPORTS SHOCK !

PM Angry

CYCLICAL

ACTIVITY 2
One of the most worrying features of unemployment in the 1970s was the apparent increase in structural unemployment. Most economists would agree that this type of unemployment can devastate a region or a whole economy and can last a very long time. This is especially true if the market mechanism is left to its own devices to adjust for the changes in the demand for different types of labour. Examine data 4.13. Describe what has happened to the different types of unemployment.

4.13

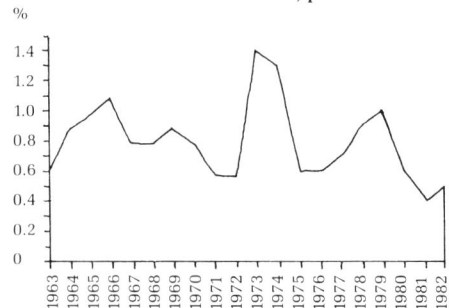
Unfilled vacancies, per cent

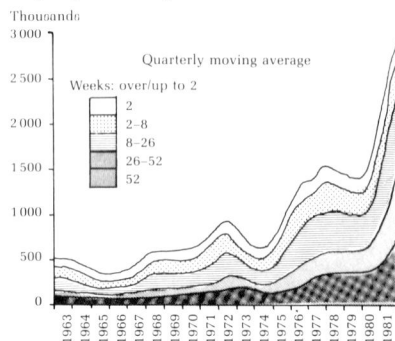
Unemployment by duration UK 1963–1981

Source: Department of Employment: Department of Manpower Services, Northern Ireland

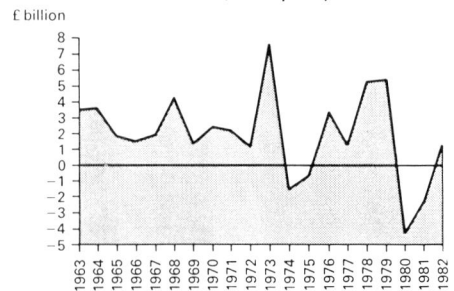
Change in gross domestic product at factor cost (at 1975 prices)

Source: Economic Trends, Annual Abstract of Statistics CSO

TASK 4   To discover the causes of unemployment.

Unfortunately, economists do not agree on the causes of unemployment and as the astute student will be aware from following current affairs, there are many political and sociological angles to the debate. There are numerous shades of economic opinion about the causes of unemployment, but as with many other macro-economic controversies, economists tend to fall into two schools of thought. On the one hand there are those who believe that, essentially, unemployment is a demand side economic problem caused by lack of spending and there are those who argue that the root cause is largely the result of supply side imperfections in the labour and goods markets, and a lack of incentives.

ACTIVITY 1

It has often been said that unemployment may result from the introduction of new technological processes. This is an aspect of structural unemployment. Consider data 4.14. Do you think that this is a demand side or supply side argument?

4.14

Workers are paid more, companies make higher profits, prices to consumers come down – the ball-point pen and the pocket calculator are two obvious examples.

People have higher purchasing power, which they use to buy more goods and services, which in turn generates more output and jobs.

Technology bogy is age-old fallacy

The arrival of the microchip has revived age-old fears that technological change will inevitably lead to ever-higher unemployment.

These fears are, happily, based on a fundamental fallacy: that there is only so much work to be done in the economy so that if fewer people are needed to produce any given output the number of jobless must rise.

This fallacy, known as the 'lump of labour' fallacy, is given the lie by all historical experience and by common sense.

It assumes that we are already producing all the goods and services we could possibly want. This is clearly a nonsense.

To see how absurd the notion of satiation is we only have to ask ourselves whether we would have any difficulty in spending, say, double our incomes.

Creating demand

From the wheel to the word-processor labour saving inventions have been accompanied – have indeed been the motive force – behind increasing economic prosperity and more employment. The reason is that technological advance creates its own demand.

Adjustment problem

There are two caveats to this rosy picture. The first is that rapid technological change creates problems of adjustment – people who lose their jobs may not have the right skills or be in the right place to take advantage of new ones appearing.

The adjustment process can thus be both lengthy and painful (though governments can often assist by, for instance, helping with retraining or relocation).

To those at the sharp end it is little comfort to be told that new jobs are springing up elsewhere.

The second is that for counter-inflation purposes governments have recently run tight economic policies which have restrained the growth of output, so that people have been displaced faster than new jobs have been created.

But this does not mean that higher productivity is the cause of unemployment. On the contrary, because productivity growth lowers costs, for any given level of inflation, it enables the economy to grow faster.

Policies to share available work around – overtime restrictions, early retirement and so on – are based on a misconception. They would if anything tend to raise the costs of employment and so make the jobless problem worse.

Source: The *Daily Telegraph* January 29 1985

ACTIVITY 2

Consider data 4.15.

A   According to the classical view, will there ever be long-term unemployment? Explain your answer. You could use demand and supply diagrams to help you.

B   How have modern mixed economies, such as Britain's, soothed the labour force, providing a safety net from Marx's 'evil capitalists'?

C   Why would Keynes have argued for international co-operation and co-ordination if unemployment were to be reduced?

D   What are the social costs implied in the monetarist analysis?

4.15

A Marxist view

Classical view
The market mechanism will adjust itself to ensure full employment of all factors of production. Supply creates its own demand; production generates enough purchasing power to give everyone a job. If the economy overproduces temporary unemployment may occur, but it will disappear once prices of goods and factors of production fall, and the economy returns to equilibrium and full employment.

Marxist view
Capitalists create unemployment by demanding bigger and bigger profits. To increase profitability and productivity and to reduce wage costs, capitalists substitute capital machinery for labour.

Keynesian view
Unemployment is the result of a lack of effective overall demand in the economy. The free market might ensure equilibrium between sales and purchases, but not necessarily at full employment. Traditional government action to cure a recession, ie cuts in spending and also reductions in imports, only makes matters worse.

Neo-classical/monetarist view
Unemployment is caused by governments who refuse to control the rate of growth of their money supply. If there is too much money in the system bidding for scarce goods and services, prices will rise. In response wages will also rise and industry will become uncompetitive. If industry is uncompetitive, unemployment will rise. In the short term, the government must squeeze inflation out of the system by reducing inflationary expectations. This may create more unemployment until wages fall sufficiently to price people back into jobs. Wages must fall because wage increases are the main component of inflation.

Source: Adapted from 'Unemployment and the economy' John McIlroy
from *Political Issues in Britain Today* B Jones
Manchester University Press 1983

ACTIVITY 3
A   Examine data 4.16 which explains the Keynesian view of unemployment. What is meant by the economy being in equilibrium?

B   Why might the equilibrium and full employment level be different? Why does unemployment exist?

4.16

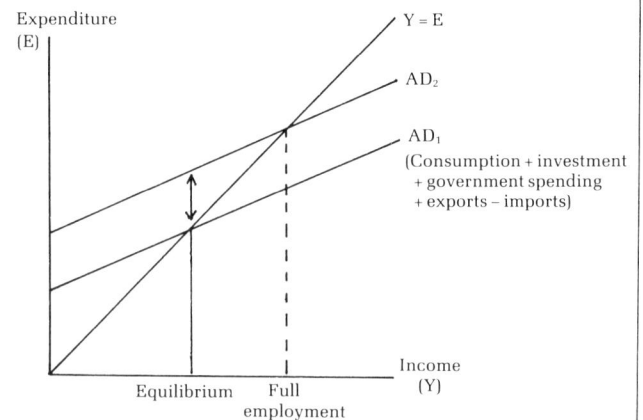

John Maynard Keynes in *The General Theory of Employment, Interest and Money* (1936) outlined the cause of unemployment as a lack of aggregate demand (spending on consumption and investment, government spending and any possible balance of payments surplus). The economy could be in a stable position (equilibrium) where national income remains the same each year because the amount of money entering the economy (injections) is the same as the money leaving (withdrawals). However simply because national income is stable, does not mean that there **has** to be enough spending to ensure full employment. Thus a deflationary gap may exist in the economy.

ACTIVITY 4

The Keynesian explanation of unemployment has been questioned in recent years. Consumption spending in Britain is buoyant. The government spends more than it withdraws from the circular flow of income; during the early to mid 1980s, when unemployment was rising fast, the UK had a balance of payments surplus. In addition, we still have inflation, which the Keynesian model suggests is unlikely when resources are under-utilised. In data 4.17 Professor Alan Budd offers an alternative view of the causes behind the rapid rise in unemployment in the early 1980s.

Explain the link between the increase in VAT in 1979, a tight monetary policy and the rise in unemployment.

4.17

The Rise in Unemployment

Unemployment rose by about $1\frac{3}{4}$ million between 1979 and 1983. The most rapid increase occurred during 1980. Such a rapid rise can only have occurred as a result of some major shock to the economy. We cannot therefore explain the rise by technical progress, which occurs at a fairly slow and steady rate, nor can we explain it by a sudden rapid rise in the size of the adult population. Most of the rise occurred because jobs were lost in manufacturing and we must try to understand why manufacturing in particular was so hard hit.

To cut a long story short, the manufacturing sector was hit by a devastating combination of a wage explosion and an appreciation of the exchange rate. We can illustrate the extent of the problem in the following way. The average manufacturing firm experienced a rise in its total costs of production (per unit) of about 25 per cent between 1979 and 1980. The largest single element of this rise was the increase in wages of over 20 per cent. There were also increases in energy costs etc. A rise of that order is not serious provided that firms can increase their prices by 25 per cent; but the rise in the exchange rate meant that if firms wanted to keep their prices in line with those charged by their foreign competitors they could not raise prices (in sterling) at all.

Faced with that shock, firms cut back production very sharply, and sacked their workers. It is not very helpful, after the event, to attribute blame for these events. My personal view is that it was a mistake to have raised VAT in the 1979 Budget, since the resulting price increases encouraged wage increases. Also it would now be generally agreed that monetary policy was unintentionally tight and that this contributed to the rise in the exchange rate.

The important point is that about 2 million jobs were lost in manufacturing. Jobs have not been created elsewhere at anything like the pace required to offset that rise in unemployment. Also the pattern of job loss has left many people without jobs ever since, hence the severe problem of long-term unemployment.

Source: *Unemployment: A Discussion Pack* Hands Across Britain 1987

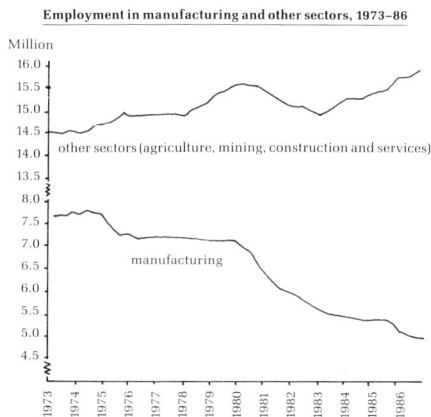

Employment in manufacturing and other sectors, 1973–86

Million

other sectors (agriculture, mining, construction and services)

manufacturing

ACTIVITY 5

Let us next consider the neo-classical view. Read data 4.18.

A What is the natural rate of unemployment?

B What, according to this idea, is the main cause of unemployment?

4.18

'. . . If people in work were to accept lower pay rises, more people would have jobs.'

Source: *Economic Progress Report* No 174 January 1985

The neo-classical view is that, in the long run, there is no such thing as involuntary unemployment and those who are registered as unemployed do so voluntarily for a variety of reasons, but largely, the neo-classicists argue, because they are not willing to accept jobs at the wage rates which jobs are on offer. They price themselves out of the market. That proportion of the labour force who choose not to work at the going wage rate is called the natural rate of unemployment. This would fall if workers were prepared to accept lower wage rates.

ACTIVITY 6
Examine the quotes in data 4.19. Write a short passage on the 'neo-classical' explanation of unemployment, incorporating these ideas.

4.19

'The natural rate of unemployment is determined by the actual structural characteristics of labour and commodity markets.'

Source: Milton Friedman

'The first and fundamental cause of unemployment is the operation of the unemployment benefit system.'

Source: Patrick Minford

'They are the prime source of unemployment.'

Source: F. Hayek commenting on Trades Unions

'The evidence suggests that, in Britain a 1 per cent change in the average level of real earnings will, in time, make a difference of between 0.5 per cent and 1 per cent to the level of employment – that will mean in all probability between 150,000 and 200,000 jobs.'

Source: Nigel Lawson

ACTIVITY 7
Data 4.20 suggests there may be a flaw in the argument that high wages cause unemployment. What is that flaw?

4.20

Source: *Global View* Birmingham Trade Union Resource Centre

TASK 5 To discover ways of reducing unemployment.

ACTIVITY 1
Read the extracts in data 4.21 which outline the Keynesian or demand side solutions to unemployment.
Can you suggest any reasons why these solutions may not work?

4.21

DEMAND SOLUTIONS

In 1955 unemployment in the United Kingdom reached its lowest peacetime level – 265,000 or 1.2 per cent of the labour force. To cut present dole queues to this level during the term of office of a government would require the creation of around 1 million additional jobs a year. Such a rate of employment creation was achieved in the early years of World War II (1938–42). Indeed it is a sobering thought that should Britain become engaged in another major (conventional) conflict, we would no doubt be back to full employment in quick time. What is required therefore is a comparable peacetime mobilisation of resources – but aimed at social rather than military objectives. The quality of jobs is no less important – ending low pay and discrimination against women and ethnic minorities has to be a priority. But these objectives can most effectively be tackled in the context of expanding employment.

Economic priorities in war time are rather straightforward – an expansion of the armed forces and of munitions production. But what would a peacetime mobilisation for full employment be *for*? What could the unemployed usefully *do*? The appalling rundown of the welfare services and basic social facilities, like housing and sewers, suggest an obvious answer. Those currently unemployed could make a tremendous contribution to the welfare of *all of us*

by the work they could carry out remedying this decay, and producing the goods and services required to eliminate the poverty of large sections of the population.

Of course there is not a perfect match between the skills and experience of those without a job and the types of work most needed. So extensive training programmes would be an absolute priority within a plan for full employment. But nobody can seriously assert that we have unemployment because there is nothing useful the unemployed could do.

We have got to reduce unemployment at least to the level of $1\frac{1}{4}$ million where it was only eight years ago. For this purpose there has to be more spending, initially by the government. But this will not create jobs if it leaks into higher inflation rather than paying for extra output.

So how can we ensure that the extra spending does not produce an upsurge of inflation, as unemployed workers become more scarce? We have to follow four basic rules.
1. *Target the extra demand towards the unemployed, the low skilled and the regions.*
2. *We should train far more of our people.*
3. *We must have an incomes policy.*
4. *We must have a sensible financial policy.*

Source: Andrew Glyn, Richard Layard *Unemployment: A Discussion Pack* Hands Across Britain 1987

ACTIVITY 2
Keynesians suggest a reflationary policy to solve unemployment. What evidence is there that this would be successful? Read data 4.22.

A Why would it be difficult for the current Conservative government to indulge in '... specific direct interventions in the market economy'?

B What theoretical case is there for paying workers on public schemes '... going trade union rates'?

4.22

WEST OF THE DOLE

With regard to policies, the successful employment countries have all pursued expansive Keynesian-type policies. The important contribution of the latter to Japanese full employment is particularly striking, much more important than the star performance of the Japanese exporters. But Keynesianism is not enough. First, successful Keynesianism has to be accompanied by consistent, congenial monetary policy, in particular of low real interest rates. Second, in all the low unemployment countries, expansive fiscal and monetary policies have been crucially supplemented by nationally specific direct interventions in the market economy.

In the Swedish case, such direct interventions have mainly taken the form of 'active labour market policy measures', of special public works and public vocational (re)training programmes, at their peak, in 1978–79, reducing unemployment by about 4.0%. The extensive vocational training programmes have been rather effective in preparing for jobs on the open market. In 1983, for example, 62% of those who had taken such programmes were employed on the open market six months later. A record effectiveness was reached in 1984, with 70% of the trainees employed after six months. Wages on public works are normally according to going trade union rates.

Source: *Marxism Today* June 1985

ACTIVITY 3

Data 4.23–4.25 explain the supply side case.

A   Explain how cuts in wages could stimulate demand?

B   Suggest ways in which wages could be cut or at least wage increases reduced? You should note that the Chancellor mentions that cuts in **real wages or earnings** can help create employment.

C   What other supply side solutions are suggested in the cartoon?

4.23

Pay and Jobs

How pay affects jobs

The basic link between pay and jobs is clear. If people cost less to employ, more of them will be employed.

There are two elements to this. First, slower growth of pay would produce more jobs for any given growth of output. That is because it would slow down the process by which work comes to be done by machines. Labour-intensive activities would become cheaper relative to capital-intensive ones, and there would be more jobs on that account.

Second, a slower growth of pay would result in a faster growth of output. Costs would be lower, so companies would find it more profitable to produce goods and services. They would want to produce and sell more. To do that, they would on average set their prices lower than otherwise, and find it profitable to do so.

Lower prices would stimulate the economy in several ways. For example, unless the government were to take offsetting action, lower prices would feed through to lower interest rates. Savings would be worth more, so people would tend to save less and spend a higher proportion of their incomes. Companies would invest more. There would be an improvement in international competitiveness, which would encourage exports and discourage imports. The public sector would be able to buy more goods and services for a given level of cash expenditure.

The Chancellor on pay and jobs

The Chancellor of the Exchequer, Mr Nigel Lawson, said in the House of Commons on 30 October 1984:—

'The evidence suggests that, in Britain, a 1 per cent change in the average level of real earnings will, in time, make a difference of between 0.5 per cent and 1 per cent to the level of employment—that will mean, in all probability, between 150,000 and 200,000 jobs.

The figures show merely broad orders of magnitude, but they are based on a careful investigation of the evidence. Moreover, I have not been talking about cuts in pay, merely about pay rising in line with prices instead of much faster.

Source: 'Pay and Jobs' *Economic Progress Report* January 1985

4.24

THE RAGGED TROUSERED PHILANTHROPISTS

'Good morning, sir.'

Hunter did not return the salutation; he had not the breath to spare, but the man was not hurt; he was used to being treated like that.

'Any chance of a job, sir?'

Hunter did not reply at once. He was short of breath and he was thinking of a plan that was ever recurring to his mind, and which he had lately been hankering to put into execution. It seemed to him that the long waited for opportunity had come. Just now Rushton & Co. were almost the only firm in Mugsborough who had any work. There were dozens of good workmen out. Yes, this was the time. If this man agreed he would give him a start. Hunter knew the man was a good workman, he had worked for Rushton & Co. before. To make room for him old Linden and some other full-price man could be got rid of; it would not be difficult to find some excuse.

'Well,' Hunter said at last in a doubtful, hesitating kind of way, 'I'm afraid not, Newman. We're about full up.'

He ceased speaking and remained waiting for the other to say something more. He did not look at the man, but stooped down, fidgeting with the mechanism of the bicycle as if adjusting it.

'Things have been so bad this summer,' Newman went on. 'I've had rather a rough time of it. I would be very glad of a job even if it was only for a week or so.'

There was a pause. After a while, Hunter raised his eyes to the other's face, but immediately let them fall again.

'Well,' said he, 'I might – perhaps – be able to let you have a day or two. You can come here to this job,' and he nodded his head in the direction of the house where the men were working. 'Tomorrow at seven. Of course you know the figure?' he added as Newman was about to thank him. 'Six and a half.'

Hunter spoke as if the reduction were already an accomplished fact. The man was more likely to agree, if he thought that others were already working at the reduced rate.

Newman was taken by surprise and hesitated. He had never worked under price; indeed, he had sometimes gone hungry rather than do so; but now it seemed that others were doing it. And then he was so awfully hard up. If he refused this job he was not likely to get another in a hurry. He thought of his home and his family. Already they owed five weeks' rent, and last Monday the collector had hinted pretty plainly that the landlord would not wait much longer. Not only that, but if he did not get a job how were they to live? This morning he himself had had no breakfast to speak of, only a cup of tea and some dry bread. These thoughts crowded upon each other in his mind, but still he hesitated. Hunter began to move off.

'Well,' he said, 'if you like to start you can come here at seven in the morning.' Then as Newman still hesitated he added impatiently, 'Are you coming or not?'

'Yes, sir,' said Newman.

Source: *The Ragged Trousered Philanthropists* Robert Tressell Panther Books 1978

4.25

ACTIVITY 4
Read data 4.26.
What advantages can you find in the combined approach outlined?

4.26

A combined approach

First and foremost, there is the need to expand demand in both the private and public sectors. There is a good deal of spare capacity in the former. Various surveys show that businessmen would be willing and able to meet demand if only it were there. In the public sector the survey evidence (plus common sense and casual observation) shows there are almost unlimited needs to be met. This suggests a requirement for a balanced expansion in both sectors.

A programme of expansion could soon run into difficulties because of a skill shortage in key sectors. It follows that part of the plan must be a strengthening of skills at all levels, not least those provided by our universities and colleges. Furthermore, if we are to be able to compete internationally, the increased effort to be devoted to skill enhancement must not be a temporary one. It has to be a permanent feature of our economy.

We must now go on from the demand side of the problem to the supply side. The government can help to solve the unemployment problem by raising its own level of expenditure. Much of this will be directed at the private sector. But employers in the mixed economy will only take on more workers if it is profitable to do so. There are considerable costs to hiring, ie taking on additional labour has some of the characteristics of capital investment. Thus, businessmen must have confidence that an expansion will be long lived. One reason why unemployment has been so persistent under existing policies has been a loss of business confidence in the future. New policies will help to remove that pessimism.

One useful supply side initiative would be to lower the marginal cost of hiring labour. That can be done by cutting the employer's National Insurance contribution. It is also likely that full employment will be approached more rapidly in the South East than elsewhere. It makes sense, therefore to cut the employer's contribution more in the Midlands and North than in the South.

Another consideration to bear in mind is that the needs of industry and the demands of much of the labour force call for much greater flexibility in working hours. Much has happened in that area already; but the tax and insurance system should certainly not discourage people, notably women and youngsters, from working part time, or from adding to their education and training.

The most important supply side consideration, however, is the fear of resurgent inflation. If a new policy succeeds in reducing unemployment by 1 million in two years, the labour market will be much more buoyant. It is probable that the trade unions will show restraint in their wage claims, especially when they reflect on how much they have suffered in the past eight years. But if wage moderation were to disappear, some form of incomes policy becomes vitally necessary.

Source: Maurice Peston *Unemployment: A Discussion Pack* Hands Across Britain 1987

SECTION 5   Public Finance

HYPOTHESIS	Fiscal policy is an effective tool for achieving government objectives.

Public finance relates to the raising of revenue by the government (through taxes), and also to public spending. Different governments have different policy objectives and will vary the levels of spending and taxation in order to achieve their goals.

TASK 1 To discover why the size and role of the public sector have been reduced.

In the 1980s nationalised industries and other assets owned by the state have been privatised, reversing a long-term trend. This has been accompanied by a reduction in government spending (as a percentage of gross domestic product), and also a reduction in government borrowing. At the same time income tax has been cut. The present debate is not new. Data 5.2 and 5.3 contrasts the views of two American economists writing over twenty five years ago.

ACTIVITY 1

Examine data 5.1–5.3 and then answer the following questions.

A   What economic problem does the cartoon illustrate?

B   How does Galbraith view the relationship between the public and private sectors?

C   Contrast Galbraith's view with that of Friedman.

5.1

5.2

THE AFFLUENT SOCIETY

The line which divides our area of wealth from our area of poverty is roughly that which divides privately produced and marketed goods and services from publicly rendered services. Our wealth in the first is not only in startling contrast with the meagreness of the latter, but our wealth in privately produced goods is, to a marked degree, the cause of crisis in the supply of public services.

The city of Los Angeles, in modern times, is a near-classic study in the problem of social balance. Magnificently efficient factories and oil refineries, a lavish supply of cars, a vast consumption of handsomely packaged products, coupled for many years with the absence of a municipal refuse collection service which forced the use of home incinerators, made the air nearly unbreathable for an appreciable part of each year. Air pollution could be controlled only by a complex and highly developed set of public services – by better knowledge of causes stemming from more public research, public requirement of pollution control devices on cars, a municipal refuse collection service, and possibly the assertion of the priority of clean air over the production of goods. These were long in coming. The agony of a city without usable air was the result.

Source: *The Affluent Society* J. K. Galbraith Pelican Harmondsworth 1962

5.3

FREEDOM AND CAPITALISM

The greater part of the new ventures undertaken by government in the past few decades have failed to achieve their objectives. The United States has continued to progress; its citizens have become better fed, better clothed, better housed, and better transported; class and social distinctions have narrowed; minority groups have become less disadvantaged; popular culture has advanced by leaps and bounds. All this has been the product of the initiative and drive of individuals co-operating through the free market. Government measures have hampered not helped this development.

Is it an accident that so many of the governmental reforms of recent decades have gone awry, that the bright hopes have turned to ashes? Is it simply because the programs are faulty in detail?

I believe the answer is clearly in the negative. The central defect of these measures is that they seek through government to force people to act against their own immediate interests in order to promote a supposedly general interest. They seek to resolve what is supposedly a conflict of interest, or a difference in view about interests, not by establishing a framework that will eliminate the conflict, or by persuading people to have different interests, but by forcing people to act against their own interest. They substitute the values of outsiders for the values of participants; either some telling others what is good for them, or the government taking from some to benefit others.

Source: *Freedom and Capitalism* M. Friedman University of Chicago Press 1962

ACTIVITY 2

During the 1980s the government has aimed to reduce the public sector borrowing requirement (PSBR). This policy is part of what is known as the medium-term financial strategy (MTFS). It is a quite different approach from the Keynesian policy of increasing public borrowing during times of high unemployment. By 1987 the government had achieved a surplus or public sector debt repayment.

Study the data extracts 5.4–5.6 and answer the following questions.

A Describe the main trends in the PSBR and the PSDR (both the total and as a percentage of GDP) between 1970 and 1990.
B According to the data, what effect will a cut in the PSBR have on interest rates?
C Contrast the government's medium-term financial strategy with the Keynesian view of public sector borrowing.
D How could the views in data 5.5 and 5.6 be used to explain the trends in the PSBR since 1970?

5.4

PSBR: The sum total borrowing requirements of central government, local authorities and public corporations.

Public sector debt repayment

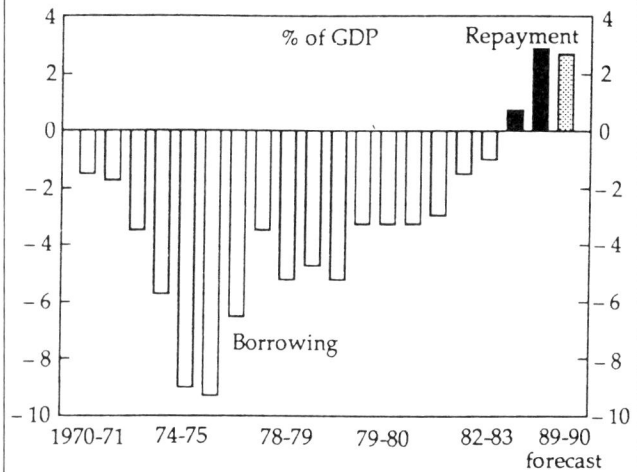

Source: *Economic Trends, Annual Abstract of Statistics* CSO

5.5

The government's medium-term financial strategy sets out a framework to 'continue reducing inflation, and to secure a lasting improvement in the performance of the UK economy.... fiscal policy is designed to be consistent with this monetary framework' and consequently 'over a period of years, a reduction in public sector borrowing, as a proportion of GDP, has a key part to play in securing a fall in interest rates.'

Source: *Financial Statement and Budget Report* (the 'Red Book') 1983–84

5.6

KEYNES

In the *General Theory of Employment, Interest and Money*, which was published in 1936, Keynes had written a book that would 'revolutionise the way the world thinks about economic problems. Keynes believed that increased spending would reduce unemployment. The mass unemployment of the thirties was a paradox. Workers needed jobs, the factories were there and people wanted goods and services. However, there was not enough spending power in the economy.

Keynes suggested that the government should make tax cuts, give subsidies and lower interest rates. If the private sector still did not respond then the government should spend the money itself.

If government spending was more than it received in taxes then it should borrow from the general public. When unemployment fell then tax revenues would rise and the original borrowing could be repaid. Government borrowing (also known as deficit financing) was not extravagant in a depression but was straightforward common sense.

Source: Adapted from *Economics of the Real World* Peter Donaldson Pelican Harmondsworth 1973

TASK 2 To discover how the UK tax system operates and how the tax revenue is spent.

ACTIVITY 1

Is the UK overtaxed? The data illustrates the size and pattern of taxation in the UK compared with seven other developed countries.

Study data 5.7 and 5.8 then answer the following questions.

A   How does the UK tax and social security contribution (as a percentage of GNP) compare with the other countries?

B   What are the main differences between the patterns of taxation and social security contributions in the different countries?

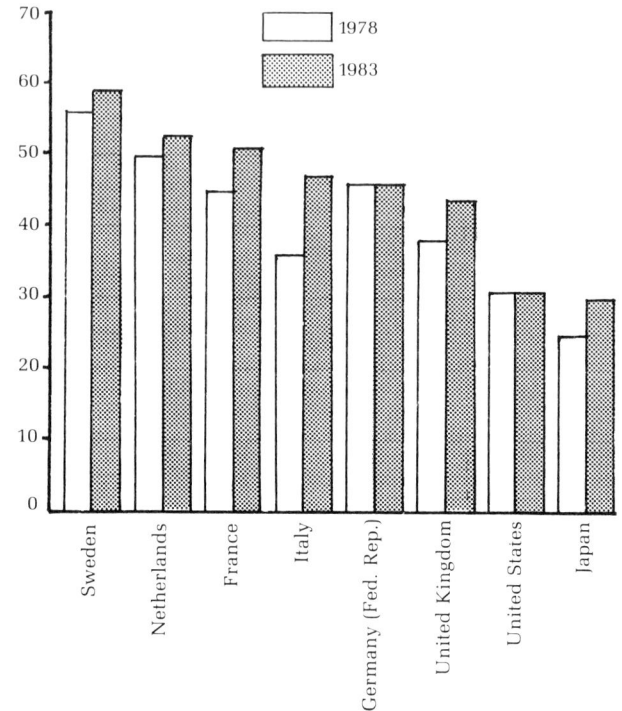

5.7

Taxes and social security contributions as a percentage of gross national product at factor cost

Source: *Economic Trends* May 1986 CSO

5.8

International comparisons of the components[1] of revenue from taxation and social security contributions[2], 1983

Percentages

	Taxes on personal income	Employees' social security contributions	Employers' social security contributions and payroll taxes	Taxes on corporate income	Taxes on property	Taxes on goods and services
United Kingdom	27.7	8.1	10.5	10.8	12.7	29.8
France	13.4	11.7	31.6	4.3	3.7	29.0
Germany (Fed. Rep.)	28.3	15.9	19.2	5.1	3.4	27.5
Italy	27.9	7.2	25.7	9.3	2.8	23.4
Japan	25.6	10.5	15.2	19.6	9.4	15.2
Netherlands	21.3	19.9	17.8	6.1	3.2	24.1
Sweden	38.9	0.0	30.3	3.4	1.7	24.4
United States	37.1	11.2	16.8	5.5	10.6	18.0

[1]The figures for each country may not total 100 per cent because of rounding and in some cases because of small amounts of taxation not covered in the table.

[2]The Figures for social security contributions exclude contributions made by the self-employed.

Source: *OECD Revenue Statistics 1965–84*

ACTIVITY 2

How has the pattern of public spending changed in the UK? The data shows changes in the level and priority of public spending. Data 5.9 shows the percentage real change in general government expenditure, ie adjusted to take inflation into account. It also shows the percentage ratio between general government expenditure to gross domestic product, ie the government's share of total national expenditure.

With reference to data 5.9–5.11 answer the following questions.

A What were the main areas of public expenditure in 1984/85?
B Describe the changes in government priorities since 1979.
C Describe and give possible reasons for the changes in general government expenditure since 1963 both in real terms and as a percentage of GDP.

5.9

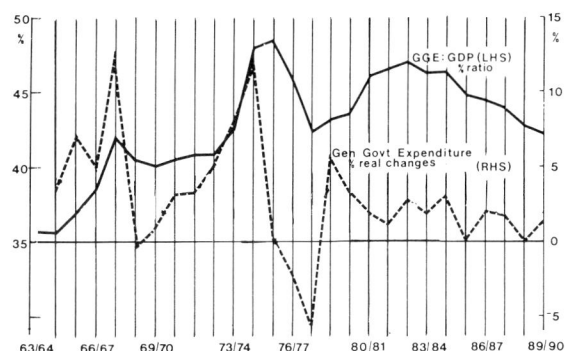

GOVERNMENT EXPENDITURE AND GDP 1963/64 - 1989/90

Source: *Lloyds Bank Economic Bulletin* February 1987

5.10

Changing priorities in public expenditure in the 1980s

	Shares of total, per cent 1984/85	Real terms changes, per cent 1979/80–1984/85
Social security	25.8	28.3
Debt interest	10.8	11.2
Defence	11.6	22.0
Education	9.4	2.1
Health	10.7	15.9
Housing	2.2	– 53.4
Transport	3.1	– 8.0
Environment	2.7	– 1.7
Home Office	3.5	30.3
Trade and industry	1.4	– 36.4
Employment	2.1	62.8
Scotland, Wales, N. Ireland	9.3	1.4
Other	7.4	14.5
Total expenditure	100	11.0
Real GDP		4.3

Source: *Lloyds Bank Economic Bulletin* February 1987

5.11

PROS AND CONS

There are many reasons why governments have tried to curb public expenditure. Too steep a rise causes either rising taxation or an increase in debt, and thus high interest rates; in either case, economic growth may suffer. It was thought in the 1970s that the public sector was preempting too many scarce resources of labour and capital, but this argument has been reversed by high unemployment creating idle resources which could be partly absorbed by public sector expansion. It should be noted that the public sector now directly accounts for only 19 per cent of the goods and services in gdp (the other 25 per cent of gdp which is public expenditure is transfers and loans) and 23 per cent of the employed labour force, compared with 23 per cent and 26 per cent ten years ago. The public sector has been blamed – not always fairly – for managing resources less efficiently than the private sector, and this has been one reason for privatization of nationalized industries and some hospital and local authority services.

There are counter-arguments for allowing the public sector to expand, at least as fast as gdp. As national income rises, so does demand for services such as health, education, and law and order.

Source: *Lloyds Bank Economic Bulletin* February 1987

ACTIVITY 3

How does the tax and benefit system redistribute income? When the rich get richer what happens to the poor? The data shows how the process of redistribution operates and also how income was redistributed between 1976 and 1986.

Study data 5.12 and 5.13 then answer the following questions.

A   Explain the difference between original, disposable and final income.

B   Describe the changes in distribution of original, disposable and final income between 1976 and 1986.

C   Discuss the case for and against a more equal distribution of final incomes. The quotes in data 5.14 may provide a starting point.

5.12

Stages of redistribution

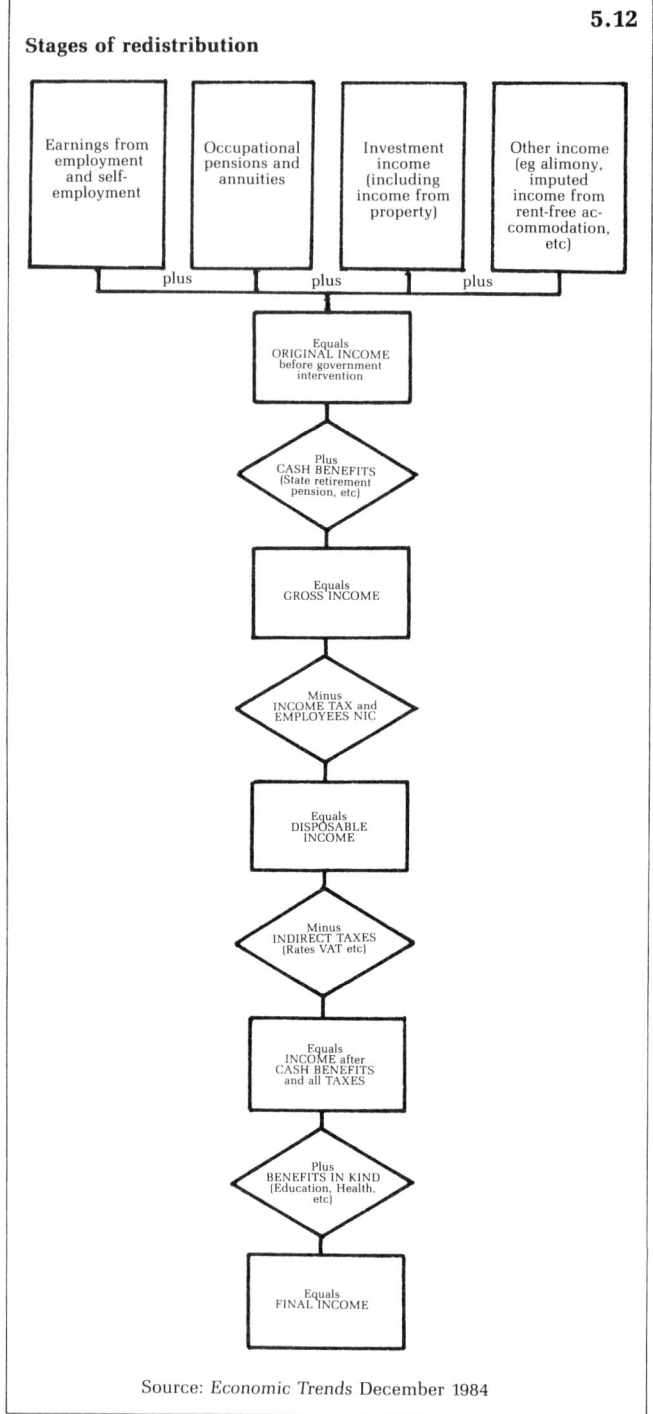

Source: *Economic Trends* December 1984

5.13

Distribution of original, disposable, and final household income

United Kingdom   Percentages

| | Quintile groups of households | | | | | |
	Bottom fifth	Next fifth	Middle fifth	Next fifth	Top fifth	Total
Original income						
1976	0.8	9.4	18.8	26.6	44.4	100.0
1981	0.6	8.1	18.0	26.9	46.4	100.0
1985	0.3	6.0	17.2	27.3	49.2	100.0
1986	0.3	5.7	16.4	26.9	50.7	100.0
Disposable income						
1976	7.0	12.6	18.2	24.1	38.1	100.0
1981	6.7	12.1	17.7	24.1	39.4	100.0
1985	6.5	11.3	17.3	24.3	40.6	100.0
1986	5.9	11.0	16.9	24.1	42.2	100.0
Final income						
1976	7.4	12.7	18.0	24.0	37.9	100.0
1981	7.1	12.4	17.9	24.0	38.6	100.0
1985	6.7	11.8	17.4	24.0	40.2	100.0
1986	5.9	11.4	17.0	23.9	41.7	100.0

Source: CSO

5.14

'From each according to his abilities, to each according to his needs.'

Source: Karl Marx

'Avarice, the spur of industry.'

Source: David Hume

ACTIVITY 4

Data 5.15 shows how taxes and benefits affect different income groups. Is income redistributed from the rich to the poor? Which taxes and benefits have the greatest effect in redistributing income?

Study data 5.15 and 5.16 then answer the following:

A Calculate the degree to which:
  ● income tax and NIC
  ● domestic rates net of rebates
  ● VAT
  ● duty on alcohol
  ● duty on tobacco
  are regressive, proportional or progressive. (Do this by calculating the amount paid in tax as a percentage of original income for each income group.)
  Describe your results.
B Calculate the degree to which:
  ● benefits in cash
  ● benefits in kind
  are regressive, proportional or progressive.
  Describe your results.

5.15

Redistribution of income through taxes and benefits, all households[1], 1983

United Kingdom   £s per year and numbers

	Quintile groups of households ranked by original income				
	Bottom fifth	Next fifth	Middle fifth	Next fifth	Top fifth
Average per household (£s per year[2])					
Original Income	120	2,580	6,880	10,570	18,640
+ Benefits in cash	3,020	2,260	1,100	750	600
Gross Income	3,140	4,840	7,980	11,300	19,240
− Income tax and NIC[3]	10	410	1,410	2,340	4,510
Disposable Income	3,130	4,420	6,570	8,960	14,730
− Indirect taxes					
Domestic rates net of rebates	220	260	310	360	450
VAT	170	310	490	640	1,040
Duty on alcohol	50	90	160	190	320
Duty on tobacco	120	140	200	190	230
Other indirect taxes	290	470	700	900	1,340
+ Benefits in kind, eg Education, Health	1,340	1,250	1,470	1,480	1,560
Final Income	3,630	4,400	6,190	8,160	12,920

[1]These estimates are based on the Family Expenditure Survey.
[2]Rounded to nearest £10.
[3]Employees' national insurance contributions

Source: CSO

5.16

Progressive tax	– a tax which takes an increasing proportion of income as income rises.
Proportional tax	– a tax wich takes an equal proportion of income as income rises.
Regressive tax	– a tax which takes a decreasing proportion of income as income rises.
Progressive	– favours the poor.
Regressive	– favours the rich.

ACTIVITY 5

What are the economic consequences when indirect taxes are imposed? An indirect tax is paid by a consumer in the form of increased prices of the taxed goods. In other words the consumer does not pay the tax direct to the government. Examples of indirect taxes are VAT (which is calculated as a percentage) and excise duty, eg on alcohol (which is calculated at a flat or specific rate). In the example in data 5.17, a specific indirect tax has been imposed.

Study data 5.17 and answer the following questions.

A   How much is consumer expenditure before and after the tax is imposed?

B   How much revenue does the producer earn before and after the tax is imposed?

C   How much is government revenue?

D   What proportion of the tax is paid by:

   ● the consumer?
   ● the producer?

E   Under what circumstances would consumers pay the biggest proportion of the tax?

   Examine data 5.18 and 5.19 and then answer the following questions.

F   Explain the possible reasons behind the view of the tobacco industry's spokesman that 'the Chancellor was destroying the industry'.

G   What factors must the government bear in mind when deciding on the imposition of a sales tax?

5.17

A Sales Tax

Evaluation of excess burdens

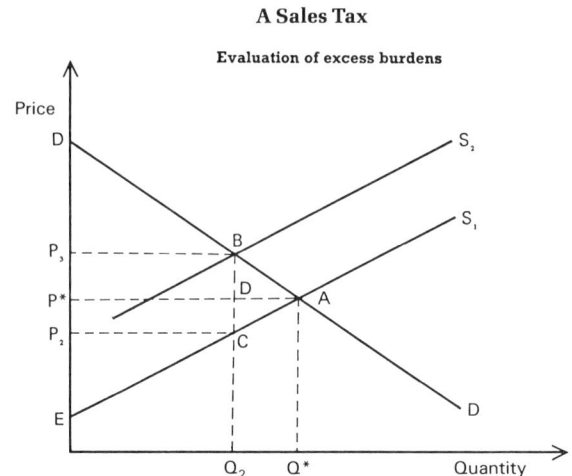

Before the sales tax is imposed the equilibrium price and quantity are P^* and Q^*. After the tax is imposed the supply curve shifts from S_1 to S_2. The new equilibrium price P_3 is higher and the new equilibrium quantity is lower. The tax paid to the government is P_3BCP_2, of which the consumer pays everything above and the supplier everything below the original price P^*.

5.18

5.19

THREE CHEERS FOR AN UNEXPECTED FREEZE

In the recent budget there was no tax increase on tobacco. It is the first time since 1978 that this has happened. A spokesman for the Tobacco Advisory Council – funded by the industry – welcomed the freeze. He claimed that previously the Chancellor was destroying the industry by imposing high taxes. The freeze would help cigarette manufacturers compete against cheap European imports. In the past three years these had captured 10 per cent of the UK market.

Officials at Philip Morris, which is a major tobacco company, said that the industry would benefit because the cheaper brands would not be pushed beyond the pocket of most smokers. Consumers had been trading down, ie buying cheaper brands and also buying less expensive, imported own label brands. The UK industry has been suffering for a number of years. Since 1974 20,000 jobs have been lost and since 1983 seven factories have closed.

The tobacco industry feels that the present price of a pack of 20 is close to the point that consumer resistance will set in. A typical price of £1.50 is made up of 112p duty and VAT and 38p which covers production costs and manufacturers' and retailers' profits.

Source: Adapted from an article by Christopher Parkes The *Financial Times* 18 March 87

ACTIVITY 6

VAT is an indirect tax that is levied throughout the Common Market. However, different countries have different rates and certain countries – the UK included – have a zero-rate for some goods. Plans to impose a common policy are being opposed by the UK.

Examine data 5.20 and 5.21 and answer the following questions.

A Why does the European Commission wish to harmonise VAT rates?

B What objections to this proposal are outlined in the articles?

5.21

BRITAIN FIGHTS VAT PLAN FOR NEW HOMES

The British Government has been taken to the European Court of Justice by the EEC Commission. The Commission claims that many goods that are zero-rated in Britain should not escape VAT. If the government loses a VAT rate of up to 15 per cent would be levied on new houses. Other goods and services that could be taxed include food, childrens' clothes, fuel and power, newspapers and books. The Commission in Brussels sees the zero-rates and exemption for new houses as an obstacle to its plans for harmonisation.

The government's case is that the VAT rates in Britain form an important part of social policy. House prices which are already rising fast in the South East will rise even faster if VAT is imposed. Home ownership is a major element of government policy and it will be claimed that this falls within the EEC rules which allow exemptions for 'clearly defined social reasons.'

Source: Adapted from an article by Alex Scott *The Guardian* September 16 1987

5.20

BATTLE LOOMING OVER BRUSSELS VAT PROPOSALS

Lord Cockfield is the European Commissioner for Internal Trade. Previously he was a member of the Conservative government. He intends to make proposals at a special meeting of the Commission that will annoy his former colleagues. His plan is to extend VAT to food, childrens' clothes and other items. Any such moves are bound to be unpopular. The intention is to harmonise VAT and excise duties throughout the EEC. This will involve squeezing all VAT rates, for all the member states, within two bands – one will be 4 to 9 per cent for necessities, the other from 14 to 19 per cent. For most of the Twelve this will require a major change in their fiscal policy. He will also call for harmonised rates of duty for tobacco, wine, spirits, beer and petrol.

The reason for these proposals is that by the end of 1992 the EEC intends to remove all internal border controls. This includes such barriers to trade as frontier checks, technical regulations and bureaucratic controls. Unless the VAT and excise duties are brought into line there will be a huge increase in fraud and smuggling.

VAT rates in EC countries, March 1987

	Reduced rate (%)	Standard rate (%)	Luxury rate (%)	Zero-rated items
Belgium	6 or 17	19	25 or 33	Minimal
Denmark	-	22	-	Minimal
France	5.5 or 7	18.6	33.3	None
W Germany	7	14	-	None
Greece	6	18	36	-
Ireland	10	25	-	Wide variety (incl. some food)
Italy	2 or 9	18	38	Minimal
Luxembourg	3 or 6	12	-	None
Netherlands	6	20	-	None
Portugal	8	16	30	Variety (incl. food)
Spain	6	12	33	None
UK	-	15	-	Wide variety (incl. food)

Source: research by Mike Kell, Institute of Fiscal Studies

Source: Adapted from an article by John Lichfield *The Independent* June 1987

ACTIVITY 7

Rates are a local property tax that successive governments have considered reforming or abolishing. They are a major source of controversy and during the General Election of 1987 the Conservatives promised to abolish domestic rates in England and Wales (having already started the process in Scotland).

Study data 5.22–5.25 and then answer the following questions.

A Outline the criticisms of rates given in the data.

B Describe how a community charge or poll tax would operate.

C Discuss the advantages and disadvantages of a community charge:
● to individuals
● to local authorities
● to central government.

5.22

'It is fairer than rates because it will spread the burden of payment more evenly. It will restore accountability by ensuring that all adults, with a few exceptions, have a direct financial stake in the spending decisions of their local councils.'

Source: Michael Howard Minister for Local Government

'The poll tax is a reactionary, regressive proposal.'

Source: Edward Heath Former Conservative Prime Minister

'The poll tax will be twice as costly as rates to collect.'

Source: Nicholas Ridley Secretary of State for the Environment

POLL TAX
HOW IT WILL AFFECT YOU

Q. WHY call it a poll tax?

A. THERE is a clear link between 18-year olds becoming eligible to vote—and going on the electoral register—and becoming liable to pay the poll tax.

Q. SO if I don't register to vote I don't pay the poll tax?

A. NOT at all. The Electoral Roll will be only one check. Local councils will make a register of properties and who lives there and may even use other local services to confirm their figures.

Q. HOW is the poll tax figure arrived at?

A. INITIALLY, the tax is intended to average £178 per head. This is based on the average level of services per person in each local authority. But obviously, that figure will vary greatly with the spending needs of local councils. In deprived inner city areas where demands are greater, people will pay more.

Labour's local government spokesman Jack Straw says the tax will vary from £93 a head in the Isles of Scilly and £131 in Rochester to a staggering £782 a head in London's Camden.

There is a North-South divide, too. In Northern industrial areas, over-18s would pay £230 to £270 each. But in the richer South it will be £140–£170 a head.

Some worried Tory MPs are rebelling against the tax because it could threaten their marginal seats.

Q. WHAT is the difference between paying rates and paying the poll tax?

A. WITH the present system you receive a single bill for your rates. But with a poll tax every adult member of the household will in effect receive a bill. So a couple with two children over 18 will pay the tax for four people.

For instance, an average rate bill in Greenwich, London is now £495. But for a family with two over-18's living at home the poll tax would total £2,432. In Southend a rates bill of £521 would go up to £736 for a family of four.

In Bury, near Manchester an average rates bill of £489 would leap to £976.

Q. Who will pay?

A. Just about everyone over the age of 18.

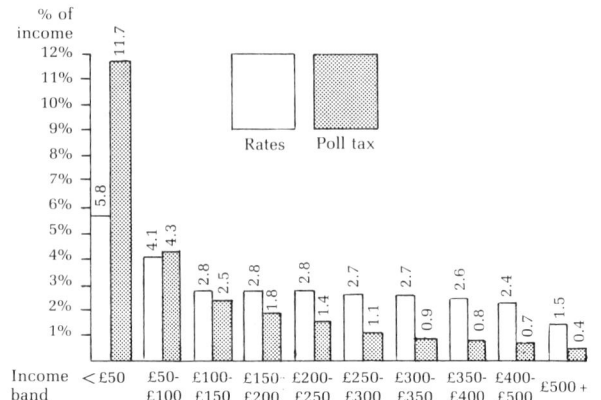

Rates and poll tax (before rebates) as percentage of household income, by income band

Source: *New Statesman* February 7 1986 Calculations by Philip Truscott, University of Surrey, based on *1981 General Household Survey.*

Q. Are there no exceptions?

A. Yes, those in old people's homes, mental hospitals or prison.

Q. Do pensioners have to pay the poll tax?

A. Yes, but the really poor will probably receive a rebate and pay only 20 per cent of the tax.

Q. What if I am unemployed?

A. Again, the poll tax applies, but you could receive a rebate.

Q. Do students pay?

A. Yes, they will be taxed by the local authority where they attend university or college.

Source: The *Daily Mirror* July 8 1987

LOCAL RATE SCRAPPING

The main objection to rates is that they are not related to ability to pay because they are levied on housing space and not on the number of members of the household or their income (domestic rates), and on premises and plant and not on profits (non-domestic rates). They are also regressive, in that they take up 4 per cent of the net income of those on £100–200 a week, but only 2 per cent for those on the highest incomes. They are not based even on property values, because rateable values were last fixed in 1973 (1985/86 in Scotland), and the poundage tax rate varies between local authorities.

Local authorities have none the less become addicted to rates as 'their' tax, without which they would be even more under the thumb of Whitehall. But rates now give the local authorities only 30 per cent of their income, compared with 47 per cent from central government grants. So rates are both too much for taxpayers to bear, yet too little to give the local authorities real independence. Domestic ratepayers give the local authorities only 12 per cent of their income; only half the electors are ratepayers (the other half are adult members of their households), and only two-thirds of ratepayers – 12m – pay rates in full, with the rest getting partial or total rebates. Rates thus fail to secure the accountability of local authorities to their electors.

The Green Paper

The Conservative government, published a Green Paper in 1981 which opened up an unbiased discussion. But by 1983 all the alternatives had been rejected, and the decision was to keep rates, but on the basis of updated capital values. After an electorally disastrous application of the 1983 white paper in Scotland, the 1986 green paper has reversed the policy with some highly controversial proposals.

The formerly rejected poll tax has been revived under the name of 'community charge'. This tax would be unlike rates in being based on population and not on households, but like rates in being unrelated to income or to services received.

Some of it might be rebated, but an irreducible 20 per cent would have to be paid. Business rates would be at a uniform poundage, but on updated capital values.

All analyses agree that the new system would result in some surprising redistributions of the rate burden.

The domestic changes would favour southern against northern households, but the non-domestic changes would favour northern against southern business, with central London at a particular disadvantage because of high rateable values.

Source: *Lloyds Bank Economic Bulletin* June 1986

TASK 3 To investigate the supply side view of direct taxation.

Direct taxes are levied on the people who actually bear the burden. In other words they are paid direct to the government from income. Supply side economists are concerned with efficiency and costs of production. In particular, they see wage costs and the labour market as being most important. They believe that fiscal policy, ie government policy on taxes and spending should be used in a way that does not hinder production in the private sector. The Laffer Curve suggests that beyond a certain point of taxation government revenue from taxes will fall. This is due to the disincentive effects of high taxes (causing people to work less) and also, possibly, due to greater tax evasion.

ACTIVITY 1
Do cuts in income tax have an incentive effect which raises national output and income? The data suggests that the evidence is unclear. Study data 5.26–5.29 and then answer the following questions.

A Describe what is meant by the 'substitution effect' and the 'income effect'.

B List the possible effects of a cut in income tax:
● for an individual
● for the economy as a whole.

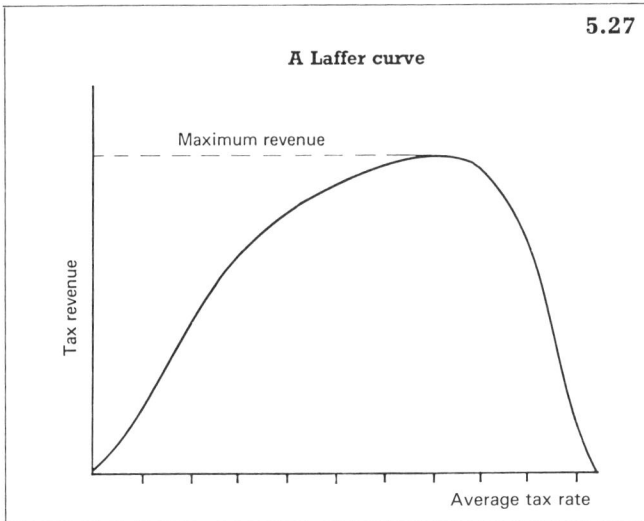

'These tax cuts really give us directors an incentive to work harder.'

Source: Adapted from *Punch* 1946

5.26

5.27

A Laffer curve

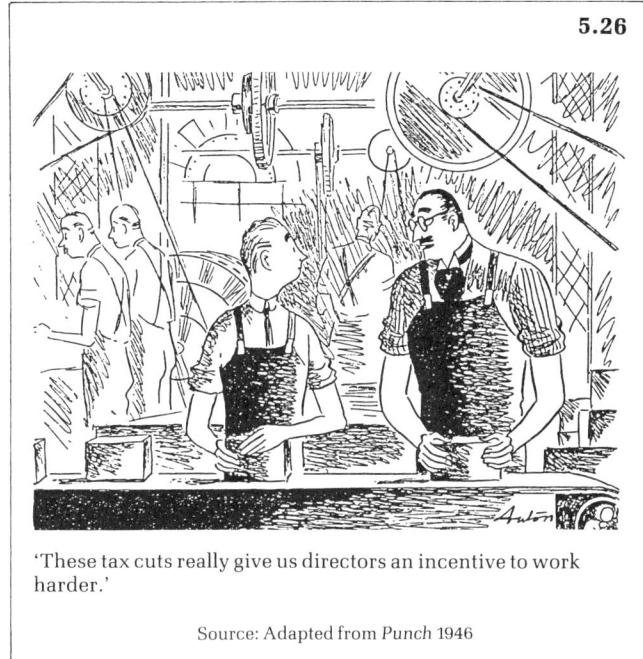

Maximum revenue

Tax revenue

Average tax rate

5.29

'If people find too big a chunk of their pay being taken away in tax they won't work so hard.'

Source: M. Thatcher

'Lower rates of tax sharpen up incentives and stimulate enterprise, which in turn is the only route to better economic performance.'

Source: Nigel Lawson Chancellor of the Exchequer

5.28
INCENTIVE EFFECT OF TAX CUTS

Professor C.V. Brown of Stirling University has been studying the incentive effects of taxation since 1979. He has recently finished his report and he concludes that there is no evidence to support the supply side view that cuts in income tax rates will improve economic performance. The incentive to work harder after a tax cut, ie to substitute labour for leisure (the substitution effect) is matched by a desire to work less hard because real income has risen (the income effect).

He found that most people – 79 per cent – are not able to vary the number of hours they work and for the rest there is only a little flexibility. However tax cuts will have an effect on demand in the economy. Keynesian theory suggests that a cut in income tax will boost disposable incomes and therefore consumption. Other things being equal, the result will be a rise in aggregate demand.

The problem with tax cuts – as a cure for unemployment – is that they are inefficient. The rise in incomes will leak out of the circular flow in the form of extra savings and extra imports.

Source: Adapted from an article by Christopher Huhne *The Guardian* January 18 1987

ACTIVITY 2

What is the poverty trap? Why is it considered a supply side problem? Data 5.30–5.32 describes how the poverty trap operates and outlines how the government plans to remedy it.

Study data 5.30–5.32 then answer the following questions.

A Which type of family is caught in the poverty trap?
B Over what range of income does the poverty trap occur (as shown on the graph)?
C Why is the poverty trap regarded as a problem?
D Describe the solution outlined in the white paper.

THE POVERTY TRAP IN 1986   5.30

The poverty trap, in its most extreme form, imposes a marginal tax rate of over 100 per cent. A family that has earned an extra £1 from work loses more than £1 in income tax and reduced benefits. The families in this position are those with children, who pay income tax and National Insurance and who receive Family Income Supplement (FIS) and Housing Benefit. Families in a similar position, but who do not receive FIS, can face marginal rates of over 80 per cent. It has been estimated that more than 250,000 families face marginal tax/benefit rates of over 80 per cent.

The government has published a Social Security White Paper which outlines some reforms to the tax/benefit system. FIS is to be replaced by Family Credit. This will be calculated on net incomes ie after tax and National Insurance have been deducted. The withdrawal rate will be 70 per cent. Similarly, Housing Benefit will be based on net income, including Family Credit and Child Benefit. The withdrawal rate will be 60 per cent. The result will be that no families will face a marginal rate of 100 per cent. However many more families will face rates at the 80 per cent level. The number will rise from 250,000 to 700,000.

Source: Adapted from 'The Poverty Trap, Tax Cuts and the Reform of Social Security' *Fiscal Studies* Dilnot and Stark February 1986
Basil Blackwell

5.31

Net weekly spending power: by level of gross earnings[1] and type of family, July 1986

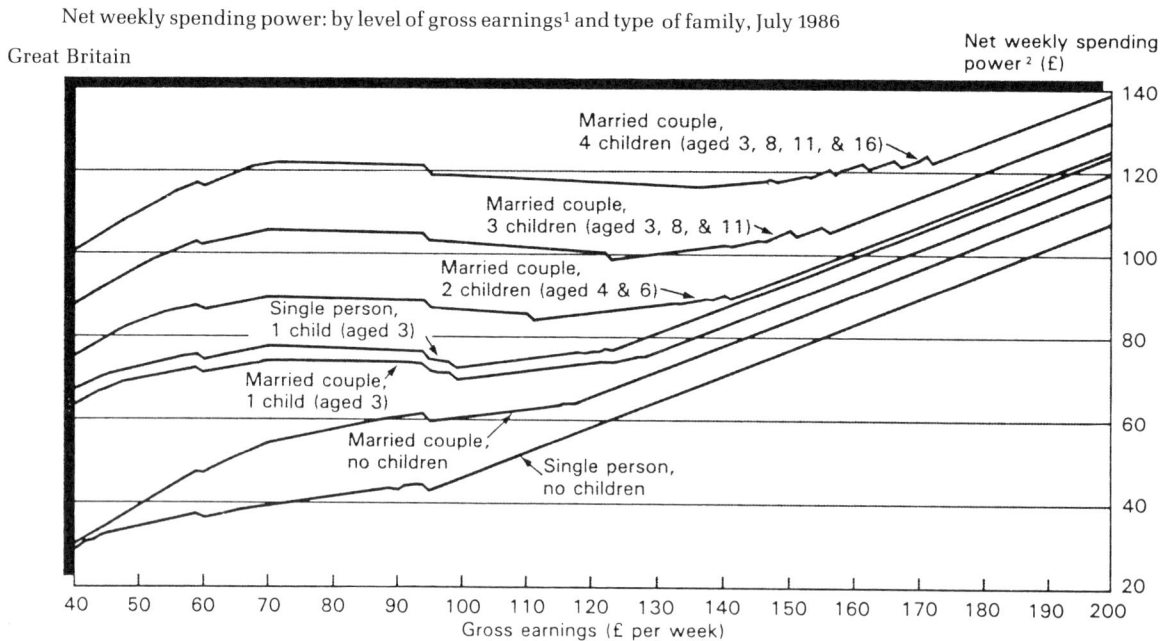

1 Gross earnings from full-time work where head of household only is in employment.

2 Gross earnings *less* deductions for tax, national insurance, rent, rates, and work expenses, *plus* receipts of all benefits which are applicable.

Source: DES

ACTIVITY 3

Having worked through all the data in this section:

A List the advantages and disadvantages of direct and indirect taxes.
B What problems could result from high rates of taxation?

NOTE   5.32

An example of a 70% withdrawal rate for Family Credit is given below. Assume that income tax is at a 27% rate. Assume that National Insurance is at a 9% rate. Therefore the combined rate is 36%. If someone who is entitled to Family Credit earns £1 extra then 44.8p of benefit will be lost $(1.00 - 0.36) \times 10.70$.

SECTION 6   Monetary Policy

HYPOTHESIS	Monetary policy is the best way to regulate the economy.

Over the last few years economists have argued about the value of monetary policy. Governments have become increasingly concerned about the money supply because of its effect on the wider economy. A number of conflicting statements give an idea of the key issues in the debate.

TASK 1   To discover some of the main issues in the debate about monetary policy.

ACTIVITY 1
Read through data 6.1 to 6.9.

A   List those statements you agree with and those you disagree with.

B   Identify any conflicting statements. Make an initial judgement as to which you consider are right and which are wrong.

C   What evidence would you need in order to evaluate the statements?

6.1

'Most people would define money in terms of coins and bank notes.'

Source: G. F. Stanlake *Macro Economics* Longman London 1979

6.2

'A major problem with the theory is that even monetarists are unable to agree on what constitutes money.'

Source: C. Huhne *The Guardian* March 10 1983

6.3

'There are three broad approaches to monetary control: direct controls, controls through interest rates and monetary base control.'

Source: R. Brown *A Guide to Monetary Policy* Banking Information Service 1982

6.4

We have found that controlling the supply of money is about as simple as getting a grip on a healthy well-greased conger eel, Anthony Harris says

Source: *The Financial Times* 8 June 1985

6.5

In a memorandum submitted to the United Kingdom Treasury and Civil Service Committee earlier this year, Professor Milton Friedman gave his design for guiding the modern economy and, as always, with clarity and succinctness.

'Inflation over any substantial period,' he said, 'is always and everywhere a monetary phenomenom, arising from a more rapid growth in the quantity of money than in output' adding that 'few economic propositions are more firmly grounded in experience – experience extending over thousands of years and the face of the globe.'

Source: J. K. Galbraith *The Guardian* October 20 1980

6.6

It is a very long time since there have been any bombshells from Oxford University quite like the one which Professor David Hendry has just dropped on Professor Milton Friedman. Friedman, the emperor of international monetarism, is roundly declared to have no clothes on.

The implications for business economists, market dealers, students, academics and governments are quite simply shattering, for no single piece of research that I can remember has so effectively undermined the monetarists' conventional wisdom that inflation is always caused by 'too much money chasing too few goods'.

Source: C. Huhne *The Guardian* December 15 1983

6.7

The economy went into a recession deeper, sharper and earlier than any other major economy, and suffered a rise in unemployment more than double that of other big industrial economies.

This was part of what ministers called a 'transitional cost' before the sun-lit uplands of low inflation, high growth, and 'more real jobs'. Meanwhile, the transitional costs have become permanent ones. And now Mr Lawson implicitly tells us that it was all a ghastly mistake.

Source: *The Guardian* October 14 1985

6.8

CHANCELLOR Nigel Lawson yesterday promised Britain a rosy future as the incentive for sticking to the Tories' tough cash clamp-down.

Regular tax cuts would be the major prize for keeping up the war on inflation.

Mr Lawson said economic recovery was now well under way and more jobs were being created.

Source: *The Sun* March 14 1984

6.9

'Effective monetary policy means cutting the money supply.'

TASK 2   To decide on a definition of money.

ACTIVITY 1
Read through data 6.10.

A   Try to write a definition of money.

B   Agree on a common definition of money with another student. Be prepared to defend your definition to others.

6.10

mon'etary (mun-), *a.* of coinage or money.
mon'éy (mun-), *n.* (pl. *moneys*), coin or banknotes. **moneyed** (mun'id), *a.* wealthy. **money-lender,** person who lends money at interest. **money order,** order for payment of money through post office, bought by sender and cashed by recipient.

Source: *The Oxford School Dictionary* Oxford University Press Oxford 1978

ACTIVITY 2
Examine data 6.11 and 6.12.

A   List the problems you feel might be experienced in a barter economy.

B   Describe how money can overcome each of these problems.

C   Do sterling bank notes fulfil the four main functions of money in all situations?

'I find this lack of confidence in sterling most disturbing.'

Source: Adapted from *Punch*

6.11

Money

1 Money is used to overcome the difficulties experienced in barter.
  (a) Establishing a double coincidence of wants—finding someone who has what you want and also wants what you have.
  (b) Agreeing on a measure of value.
  (c) Wanting to store some of the value of a good for later use, ie the need to be able to store wealth.
  (d) Problems associated with transporting goods to an agreed market place.
2 Money is therefore required to fulfil four main functions.
  (a) *Medium of exchange*—a half way stage in the process of exchange, eg a worker exchanges his labour first for money (his wages) and then exchanges this money for goods and services.
  (b) *Unit of account*—a measuring rod of value, eg it is usual to talk of a *Toblerone* costing 2 Swiss Francs or 65 pence rather than 2 loaves of bread.
  (c) *Store of wealth*—money allows some of the value of a good which has been traded to be stored for later use, eg a worker does not have to spend all his income immediately, some can be saved and used at a later date.
  (d) *Standard for deferred payments*—money allows contracts to be signed and for payments to be made at some agreed later date.

Source: *A Guide to A Level Economics* A Tebitt Nelson Surrey 1986

ACTIVITY 3
Read through data 6.13.

A Link each characteristic of money described with a function it helps to fulfil.
   Add any other characteristics you feel would help money to fulfil its functions.

B Place the functions and characteristics of money in order of importance.
   Discuss your list of priorities with another student. Do any differences occur? Why?

ACTIVITY 4

A Write a definition of money following activities 2 and 3. Compare this to your definition in activity 1.

B Prepare a definition of money, perhaps with another student, on a sheet of a flip chart or sugar paper. This definition could be shown to others and challenged in group discussion. Following a discussion, individuals should write up their own definition of money.

ACTIVITY 5
In this task you have examined some of the problems of achieving a satisfactory definition of money.
In your opinion, can anything act as money? Do you think money essential in all economic systems?

6.13

The characteristics of money
In theory, anything can act as money. In the past, everything from cowrie shells, to pigs, to cigarettes have been used. It helps, however, if what acts as money has certain *characteristics* or features. These include:

● *limited supply* – this means that there must be only a limited amount of money available. If it were not limited, it would not have any value. So gold is a good money in this sense, whereas sand would be very poor.

● *divisibility* – it is easier if the money can be broken down into small units. Pigs were not very useful as money, because it is not possible to chop off a small part of the pig to make a payment and keep the pig intact.

● *portability* – it should be easy to carry around.

● *durability* – it should last. Cigarettes, for example, are not a very good form of money, because they deteriorate quickly when passed from person to person.

● *homogeneity* – money of the same value should be the same in size, shape etc.

Without money, the whole system of the division of labour, specialisation and exchange would collapse. Money is therefore a very important resource in the economy.

Source: *Economics for GCSE* Alain Anderton Collins Educational London 1986

TASK 3 To discover how changes in the money supply can be measured.

The government has used a number of measures of money over the past few years. Your task is to look at each of the measures and evaluate them. Try to decide which, if any, is the best measure. Begin by writing your own definition of money.

ACTIVITY 1

A Would £1 coins be a good measure of the amount of money in the economy?

B How would you go about measuring changes in the number of £1 coins in circulation?

'What kept me? £50,000 in £1 coins – that's what!'

Source: Adapted from The *Daily Express* November 15 1984

ACTIVITY 2

A Read through the article, Why some money is more 'moneyish'.
Using your own definition of money, group the items mentioned by the writer into those things you think are money and those things you think are not money.
Justify each choice.

B Compare your answers to A with those of another student. Discuss any differences.

6.15
WHY SOME MONEY IS MORE 'MONEYISH'

To understand about money you need to grasp the fact that some money is more 'moneyish' than others. Money in our pockets, the notes and coins, is definitely money. It can be spent straight away without having to go to the bank to draw it out. Money in a current account at a bank is also money, but you could say that it is not quite as 'moneyish' as notes and coins. Try giving a taxi-driver a cheque! This can be taken further. To pay a bill out of a bank deposit account or a building society account you would need to give some notice.

There are also other types of savings that are not really money at all. Financial assets like stocks and shares and government securities have to be changed into money before you can buy anything with them.

There is no clear line between money, near money and financial assets that are not money at all. If you have £50 in your pocket it is money. Put it in a bank current account and it is still probably money. Under some definitions it would continue to be money if you put it into a building society account. Buy shares with it and it stops being money altogether. It doesn't suddenly stop being money. As it has become more difficult to buy something with it the £50 has gradually got less 'moneyish'.

Source: Adapted from an article by Hamish McRae *The Guardian* March 8 1979

ACTIVITY 3
Data 6.16 describes eight different measures of money. Choose the measure which you feel best represents money and explain why you have chosen it.
Why do you think there is more than one measure of money?
(Data 6.17 may help you with activity 3.)

6.16

Measures of money

M0	Notes and coin in circulation with the public and held by the banks plus banks operational deposits held at the Bank of England. Operational deposits are total deposits held at the Bank of England less the volume required in order to satisfy the officially imposed cash ratio.
M1	Notes and coin in circulation with the public plus sterling sight deposits held by the UK private sector with the monetary sector.
Non-Interest M1 (NIM 1)	M1 excluding those sight deposits which pay interest.
M2	Notes and coin in circulation with the public plus sterling cheque accounts plus retail deposits, ie sums of £100 000 or less with a maturity of one month or less held by the UK private sector with UK banks, building societies, and in the National Savings Bank Ordinary Account.
£M3	Notes and coin in circulation with the public plus *all* sterling bank accounts (including certificates of deposit) held by UK residents in the private sector with the monetary sector.
M3c	£M3 plus private sector holdings of foreign currency bank deposits.
M4	£M3 plus private sector holdings of building society shares and deposits and sterling certificates of deposit minus building society holdings of bank deposits and bank certificates of deposit, and notes and coins.
M5 (PSL2)	M4 plus holdings by the private sector (excluding building societies) of money-market instruments (bank-bills, Treasury bills, local authority deposits) certificates of tax deposit and national savings instruments (excluding certificates, SAYE and other long-term deposits.)

Source: D. T. Llewellyn 'The Difficult Concept of Money', p. 19. *Economic Review*, Vol. 2 No. 3 January 1985 and *Bank of England Quarterly Bulletin*, 1987

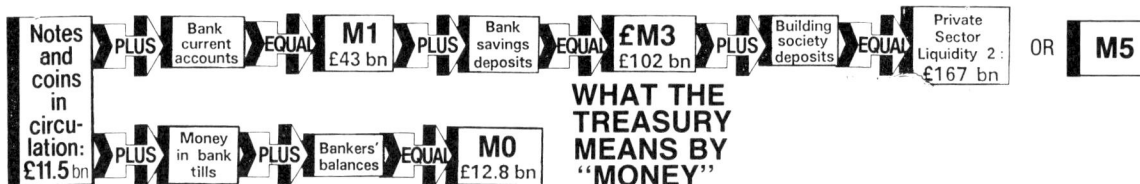

6.17

WHAT THE TREASURY MEANS BY "MONEY"

Source: *The Guardian* March 14 1984

ACTIVITY 4
Read the article extract in data 6.18.

A What do you think is meant by the terms base money, narrow money and broad money?

B Categorise each of the measures in data 6.16 into either base money, narrow money and broad money.

C Do the measures fit easily into the three categories?

D Do you agree with the writer that 'monetarism is not even past the first base of definition'?

E A class activity could be to agree on a common classification of money for each of the three types.
Half the class could defend the proposition that 'it does matter if there is more than one measure of money'. The other half of the class could oppose it.

6.18

The milky way of monetary indicators

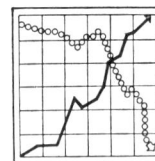

ECONOMICS
Christopher Huhne
Nearly a year and a Budget ago, the Chancellor finally did what he had sworn he would never do: he raised his monetary target by a full four per centage points. He also added to what had been the pole star of his policy, a milky way of other indicators, including the exchange rate, and thus confirmed the deep misgivings which existed about the course of policy since 1979. So what, as the Chancellor prepares his fifth Budget on Tuesday, is left of Britain's monetarist experiment?

A major problem with the theory is that even the monetarists are unable to agree on what constitutes money. There are basists, who would count only notes and coin (M0). There are narrow money men who add in chequing accounts at banks (M1). There are broad money men who include deposit accounts and even building society accounts (sterling M3 and PSL2). Suddenly, monetarism is not even past the first base of definition.

Source: *The Guardian* March 10 1983

ACTIVITY 5

A Describe what has happened to each of the measures of money shown in data 6.19 and 6.20.

B What implications do the trends have for monetary policy?

C Prepare a report on a particular measure comparing it to one of the other measures and explaining differences in behaviour.
Discuss your report with other students.

6.19

Recent growth rates of £M3, M4, and M5
Twelve-month growth rates: *not seasonally adjusted*

End-period	£M3	M4	M5
1981	13.7	13.8	12.5
1982	8.9	11.9	12.0
1983	10.3	12.8	12.6
1984	9.6	13.3	12.9
1985	13.4	13.0	12.6
1986	18.0	15.2	14.5

Source: *Bank of England Quarterly Bulletin*, May 1987

6.20

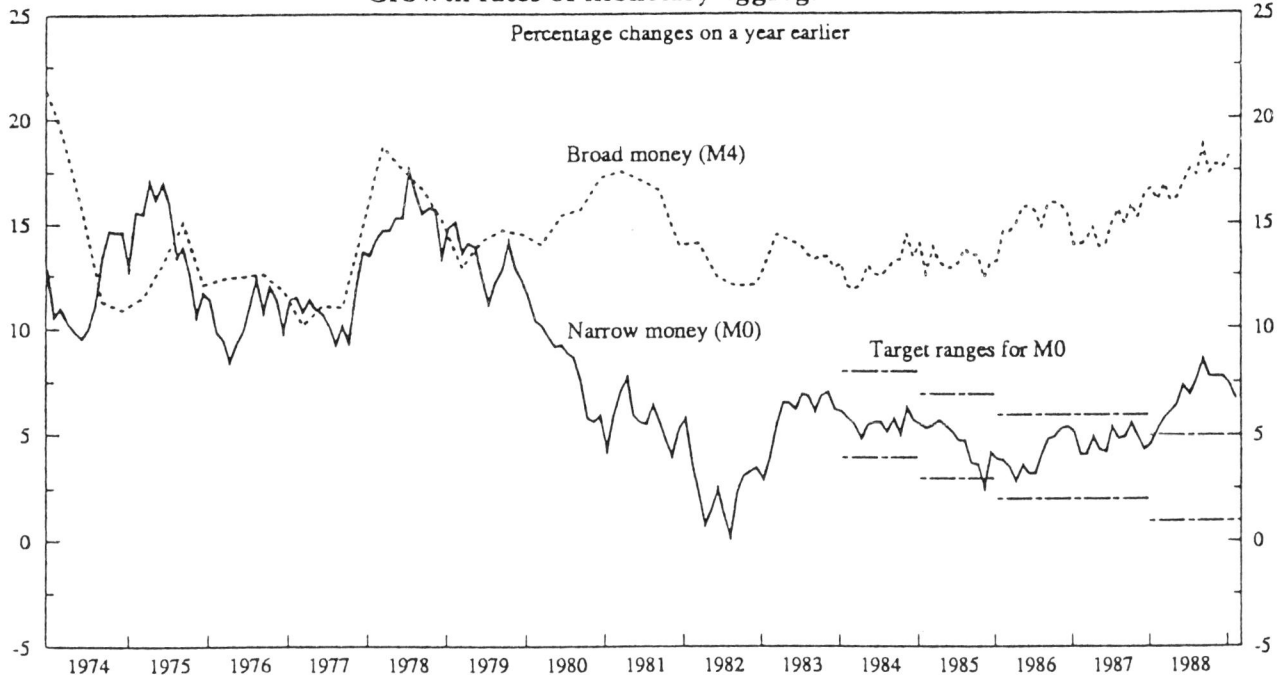

Growth rates of monetary aggregates
Source: 1989 *Medium Term Financial Strategy* Treasury

ACTIVITY 6
Read data 6.21.

In this section you have examined some of the problems associated with trying to measure the money supply.

What characteristics would a good measure of money have? Do you think the UK has a good measure of money?

6.21
ECONOMIC COMMENTARY

I have not dared to confuse the issue with the rather important question of what is money. But as the American economist Kenneth Bolding put it some years ago at a dinner in honour of Milton Friedman:
We must have a good definition of money,
For if we have not, then what have we got?
A Quantity Theory of God knows what.
And that would be almost too true to be funny.

Rodney Lord

Source: *The Times* 1978

TASK 4   To discover how economists have described the relationship between the money supply and other variables and to evaluate these theories against the evidence.

ACTIVITY 1
Read through data 6.22.

A   What is the Fisher equation?

B   How do both sides of the equation equal total money spending?

C   If velocity of money and transactions are constant, what would happen to prices if the money stock was doubled?

D   How do monetarists justify the claim that transactions are 'pretty much constant'?

6.22

After four Budgets, does monetarism add up?

The theory started from the Fisher equation, which is one of the simplest in economics, so bear with it. It says that $MV = PT$, or merely that money stock (M) times the speed at which the money changes hands (V or velocity) equals the price of goods and services (P) times the number of goods and services (T or transactions).

This equation is uncontroversial. It is true at all times and in all places. It is just an accounting identity. Both sides of the equation equal total money spending, because V is defined as the number by which you need to multiply M to get total money spending (GDP on the expenditure measure).

But the monetarists went on to claim two things. The first was that V was reliably constant. Because velocity was stable, a change in M therefore changes total money spending. Secondly, T was also pretty much constant in the long run because output or real spending (which equal each other) were determined by real things like labour skills and natural resources. The economy had a natural tendency to seek an equilibrium of full employment of men and machines without help from government policy.

Clearly, if V and T were constant or determined by other factors then a change in the money stock (M) over and above the change in T would lead to a change in prices (P). You just had to stop printing money.

Source: *The Guardian* March 10 1983

ACTIVITY 2
Examine data 6.23.

A   According to these figures is V reliably constant between 1970 and 1977?
Is T reliably constant during the same period?

B   How constant would the figures have to be to justify the description 'reliably constant'?

C   Does $MV = PT$? Use figures for three years to illustrate your answer.

D   Is there a relationship between M and P?

E   Use the data you have encountered so far to prove the theory that $MV = PT$. (A time lag could exist, the measure of money could be challenged.)
Use the data to disprove the theory.

6.23

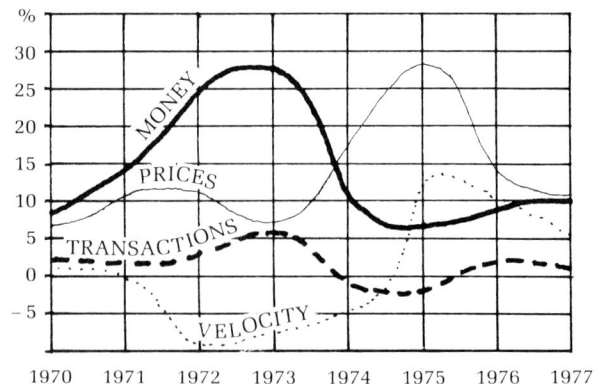

Source: Adapted from *The Times* 1978

ACTIVITY 3

A According to the article in data 6.24, how did Keynes say increases in money supply would affect the economy?

B How would monetarists describe the relationship between money supply and the economy?

C Which of the theories do you agree with, the Keynesian or monetarist?
Justify your choice.

ECONOMIC COMMENTARY

6.24

Miracles from monetarism but faith still needed

Although his name has been applied to the opponents of monetarism Keynes himself certainly did not think that money was unimportant. He believed rather that changes in financial conditions operated on the real economy mainly through interest rates. If money supply increased people would buy more financial assets such as gilt-edged securities and interest rates would fall. Lower interest rates would encourage higher investment and so higher output. Since large changes in money supply might be compatible with only small changes in interest rates it made more sense to act directly on interest rates.

Monetarists believe that an increase in the money supply encourages people not only to buy more financial assets but also to buy goods. There is therefore a direct effect from a change in money supply on the level of activity and, as we approach full capacity, on the level of prices.

Source: *The Times* 1978

ACTIVITY 4

Read data 6.25 and 6.26.

A Is the cartoon in data 6.25 most likely to represent a monetarist or Keynesian point of view? Explain your answer.

B What would be the effect of an increase in demand from
  ● a Keynesian point of view?
  ● a monetarist point of view?

6.25

'Apparently there is too much money around.'

6.26

Whereas Keynesians believe that the main influences on the price level are external factors such as trade union power, monetarists believe that the 'given' factor is the level of employment which the economy is capable of providing at any one time. In other words for Keynesians a boost to demand (and thus an increase in the money supply) will mainly affect output while for monetarists its main effect will be on prices.

Source: Adapted from *The Times* August 24 1987

ACTIVITY 5
Read data 6.27.

A How do 'rational expectations' monetarists say money supply affects wages and prices?

B Why does the writer say it is a theory which cannot be proved wrong?
Do you think this writer supports or opposes monetarists?

C How could money supply affect sterling? Why would this feed through to prices?

D Prepare flow charts showing the effects of increases and decreases in the money supply according to 'rational expectations' monetarists and the London Business School. This could be completed with another student.

6.27

The theory that cannot be proved wrong

ECONOMICS   Christopher Huhne

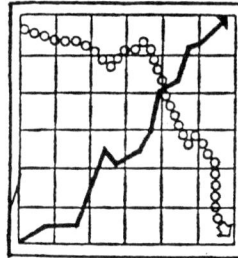

When asked to explain how the money supply affects inflation, 'rational expectations' monetarists say that if people believe the government is in control of the money supply wage demands will fall and so will costs and prices. The advantage of this theory is that it cannot be proved wrong. If inflation increases despite monetary control it is because people believe the Chancellor wasn't controlling the money supply. If inflation falls even though money supply is increasing, it is because people thought the Chancellor was in control. The London Business School also have a theory as to how the money supply affects inflation. They say that tighter controls on money supply increase interest rates which attracts footloose international funds. This boosts sterling and import prices rise more slowly. Competition forces British companies to raise their prices slowly as well. Thus inflation is reduced.

Source: Adapted from an article by C. Huhne *The Guardian* March 10 1983

ACTIVITY 6

A List the theories presented in data 6.24, 6.26 and 6.27.

B Use the evidence in data 6.28 to evaluate these theories.
What other information would you need to decide if each of the theories was valid or not?

ACTIVITY 7
In this section you have examined some of the theories describing the relationship between money supply and the economy.
How might an increase in the money supply affect the UK economy?

6.28

Income, prices, money and unemployment

Year	GDP at factor cost, current prices £ billion	GDP at factor cost at 1980 prices 1980 = 100	Retail Price Index 1975 = 100	£M3 £ billion	Unemployment (000s) excluding school leavers
1971	50.0	86.0	59.3	19.0	774.0
1972	55.9	88.2	63.6	24.1	826.1
1973	65.3	94.7	69.4	30.6	591.2
1974	75.6	93.2	80.5	34.0	590.9
1975	95.8	92.1	100.0	36.0	902.3
1976	113.8	94.6	116.5	39.5	1229.4
1977	129.1	97.0	135.0	43.2	1313.0
1978	148.7	99.9	146.2	49.9	1299.1
1979	171.0	102.4	165.8	56.5	1227.4
1980	199.3	100.0	195.6	67.1	1560.8
1981	218.0	98.7	218.9	83.7	2419.8
1982	235.8	100.8	237.7	91.5	2793.4
1983	257.5	104.1	248.6	101.2	2969.7
1984*	264.2	106.0	260.3	106.3	2979.0

*All figures for second quarter: GDP given at annual rate
From 1981, figures for £M3 calculated on new basis

Source: *Economic Trends Annual Supplement 1984 and 1985* CSO

TASK 5   To discover how the government has tried to control the money supply and to evaluate the effectiveness of these controls.

ACTIVITY 1
Read data 6.29.

A   What do you think is meant by 'ceilings on lending'?

B   How could 'qualitative guidance' affect the economy?

C   If you were given the task of reducing hire purchase borrowing, what kinds of controls might you impose?

6.29
The early controls
During the 1950s and 1960s credit was controlled by putting ceilings on the growth of lending by individual banks. After being initially imposed only on the clearing banks they were extended to other financial institutions.

As well as ceilings, the Bank of England quite often gave instructions to banks on which sector of the economy they could lend to. This qualitative guidance told banks to give priority to lending to parts of the economy that were thought to be important such as investment in industry and for the production of exports. Hire purchase agreements to consumers were often restricted as well.

Source: Adapted from *A Guide to Monetary Policy* R. Brown Banking Information Service 1982

ACTIVITY 2
Read data 6.30.

A   What would be the advantages of nationalising the clearing banks so they were owned by the government? What would be the disadvantages?

B   Do you think a political party would be elected on such a manifesto?

C   A class activity could be to debate the motion – 'This house believes that the banks should be nationalised.'

Source: The *Observer* 1982

ACTIVITY 3
Examine data 6.31 and 6.32.

A   Why would banks be reluctant to increase their deposits above the corset limit?

B   What do you think is meant by 'interest-bearing deposits'?

C   Was the corset an effective way of controlling the money supply?

D   Do you think the three channels of leakage were significant?

6.31
Figures foul-up leaves analysts with egg on their faces
Frances Cairncross finds where the money supply sums went wrong
With the end of the corset the Bank of England statisticians have found three ways it may have leaked.

First, with the removal of exchange controls banks were able to lend through their foreign branches in faraway places such as Luxembourg and the Canary Islands without affecting their credit limit.

Second, banks issued acceptances instead of money. This was a way of guaranteeing a loan to a company without lending cash itself. The leakage through this channel is estimated at two billion pounds.

Third, local authorities borrowed from companies when banks' lending was restricted. This kind of borrowing doesn't affect the money supply but does add to demand. The sheer scale of this leak has taken the Bank of England by surprise.

Source: Adapted from *The Guardian* August 12 1980

6.32
THE CORSET – A DIRECT CONTROL
This was introduced in December 1973 to set a limit on how fast banks interest bearing deposits could grow. If the growth was above the limit, banks had to deposit some of their money at the Bank of England. Since no interest would be paid on these deposits the banks stood to lose if they lent too much money to their customers. The corset was finally abolished in June 1980.

ACTIVITY 4
Examine data 6.33–6.35.

A   What is the rate of interest and why is it charged on loans?

B   Do you think that the interest rate offered on loans is an important factor in borrowing? What other factors are important?

C   How would an increase in interest rates affect:
● the government
● firms
● consumers?

6.33

RATE OF INTEREST
The price of borrowed money. If a sum of money is borrowed for a specified period of time, the amount which is repaid by the borrower to the lender will be greater than the amount which was initially lent.

Source: Penguin *Dictionary of Economics* G. Bannock, R. E. Baxter, R. Rees Penguin Harmondsworth 1986

6.34

The rate of interest in the economy may affect the level of borrowing. If a rise in interest rates reduces the amount of money borrowed by firms, government and consumers, then the supply of money will be restricted.

6.35

Source: Swift Finance

ACTIVITY 5
Read through the article in data 6.36.

A   Which is the largest area of bank lending?

B   According to the article what would be the effect of increased interest rates on output?

C   How might inflation increase company borrowing?

6.36

ECONOMIC NOTEBOOK
by FRANCES CAIRNCROSS

The bulk of bank lending is to industrial and commerical companies. Can the Government, they ask, control bank lending directly by changing the level of interest rates?

The short answer is 'not much, and not quickly.' High interest rates (in real terms) may eventually reduce companies' borrowing, but only after they have pushed firms into cutting back on employment, production or stocks.

That will reduce their demand for working capital. But in the 'short to medium run,' the amount companies borrow seems to be mainly determined by their demand for working capital, and inflation will increase that by increasing production costs.

Now this is not the same thing as saying that the Government cannot control the growth of the money supply. But it does suggest there is a lot of what car buffs would call 'loopy link' in the system.

That the impact of high interest rates on bank lending is slow and uncertain is something which the Bank of England has publicly acknowledged already. Indeed the June issue of the Quarterly Bulletin contained a table which showed the quarterly increase in bank lending to industrial and commerical companies growing by 1.6 per cent in the third quarter of 1979; by 3.1 per cent in the fourth quarter; and by 8.1 per cent in the first quarter of this year. QED, one might say.

Source: *The Guardian* July 12 1980

ACTIVITY 6

Data 6.37 shows the rate of interest charged by the Bank of England compared to the money supply from 1971 to 1980.

A   Describe the changes in Bank rate during this period.

B   How does Bank Rate compare with money supply during this period?
Is there a relationship between the interest rate and money supply?

C   Were there any other controls on money supply during the period shown?
Refer to data 6.31 and 6.32.

6.37

Bank rate/Bank of England's minimum lending rate to the market

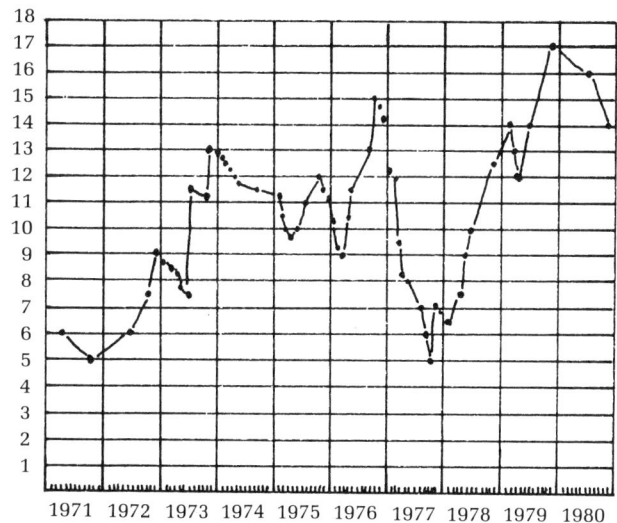

MONEY SUPPLY

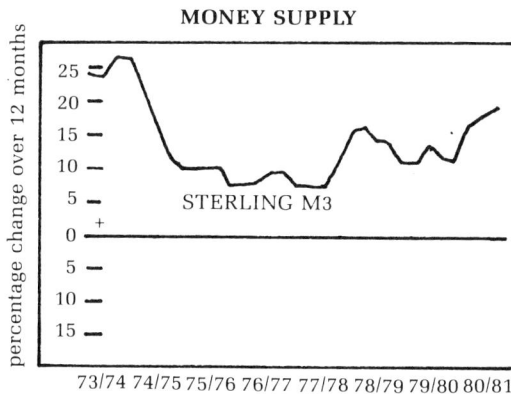

STERLING M3

73/74 74/75 75/76 76/77 77/78 78/79 79/80 80/81

Source: *Economic Trends* CSO

ACTIVITY 7

Examine data 6.38.

A   What is the PSBR? Data 6.39 may help you.

B   What has happened to the PSBR since 1970?

C   Is there any relationship between the money supply £M3 and the PSBR?

THE MONETARY SECTOR

One of the basic assumptions underlying government policy since 1979 has been that excessive monetary growth results from government borrowing. Under this assumption it is necessary to control the public sector borrowing requirement if monetary growth (and hence inflation) is to be kept in check. The graph shows how the PSBR has changed over time and also to what extent it is related to the growth in the money supply, as measured by the change in the sterling M3 figures.

6.38

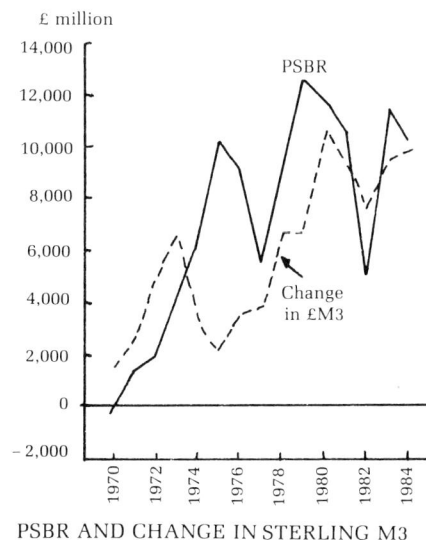

PSBR

Change in £M3

PSBR AND CHANGE IN STERLING M3

Source: *Economic Review.* Exam Special

ACTIVITY 8

Study data 6.39 and 6.40.

A   Why might the government increase the PSBR?
    In what way might this affect the money supply?

B   Is it possible for the government to cut taxes and the PSBR?

C   What costs might be involved in cutting the PSBR?

'Hasn't anyone told him about the defence cuts?'

Source: Adapted from Punch

ACTIVITY 9

Examine data 6.41 and 6.42.

A   What is meant by a money supply target?

B   What did Nigel Lawson say was wrong with sterling M3?

6.42

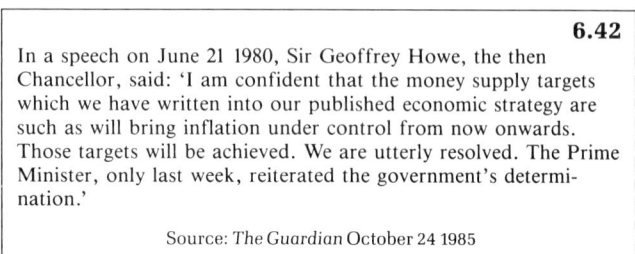

In a speech on June 21 1980, Sir Geoffrey Howe, the then Chancellor, said: 'I am confident that the money supply targets which we have written into our published economic strategy are such as will bring inflation under control from now onwards. Those targets will be achieved. We are utterly resolved. The Prime Minister, only last week, reiterated the government's determination.'

Source: The Guardian October 24 1985

6.39

POLITICAL PRESSURES ON THE MONEY SUPPLY

Firm political commitment

Firm political commitment will be needed. This may prove elusive because of the conflict between the Conservatives' pledge to cut taxes and monetary restraint. Tax reductions increase the Budget deficit – or, as it is more technically known the Public Sector borrowing Requirement. Unfortunately, this leads to problems for monetary control.

If the PSBR cannot be financed by sales of debt, typically gilt-edged securities, to the public or long-term savings institutions, the government has to borrow from the banks. This raises bank deposits and the money supply.

Indeed, if the government wants to slow down monetary growth, the PSBR will have to be lowered quite sharply, not increased. How, then, can the tax reductions promised to the electorate be reconciled with the monetary deceleration promised to the financial markets?

There are two answers

There are two answers – cuts in public expenditure and the build-up of tax revenues from North Sea oil in the early 1980s. The first may turn out to be rather painful to effect, while the second will come into the government's hands almost like manna from heaven.

But, in both cases, there will be political pressures for a relaxation of financial control and for an increase in the PSBR.

Spending ministers will haggle with the Treasury over plans for cuts, while short-term popularity may be sought by using the North Sea bonus for income tax 'give-aways.'

A strong barrier for resisting these pressures would be created if Sir Geoffrey Howe were to pledge medium-term targets for both the money supply *and* the PSBR in his first Budget.

Source: *The Guardian* May 24 1979

6.41

If you don't like the figures – rub them out

NIGEL LAWSON'S Mansion House speech did not disappoint his audience. It gave some important clues about how the Treasury intends to conduct interest rate policy, together with some cheeky re-writing of monetary history.

Mr Lawson suspended this year's target for sterling M3, the broad money measure which includes notes, coin and bank accounts and which is the only money measure to have been targeted in every year since the beginning of the ill-fated Medium Term Financial Strategy in the 1980 Budget.

He said he would reset a target for sterling M3 in the next budget, but for the moment it was not a good indicator and so he proposes not to take seriously its current 18 per cent annualised growth since February (compared with a 5.9 per cent target range). That was a political admission which the opposition seems so far to have been slow to grasp.

After all, it was on the altar of this very same monetary statistic that large swathes of the British economy – particularly manufacturing – were sacrificed in 1980 and 1981. Now Mr Lawson tells us that he will not be bothering to rein it back in because it would not be convenient. It is the nearest any Thatcherite minister has yet come to admitting the policy errors of the last six years.

Source: *The Guardian* October 24 1985

ACTIVITY 10

A Using the information in data 6.43 and 6.44 explain whether the growth in money supply has kept within government targets. Which was the worst period for control? Which was the best period?

6.43

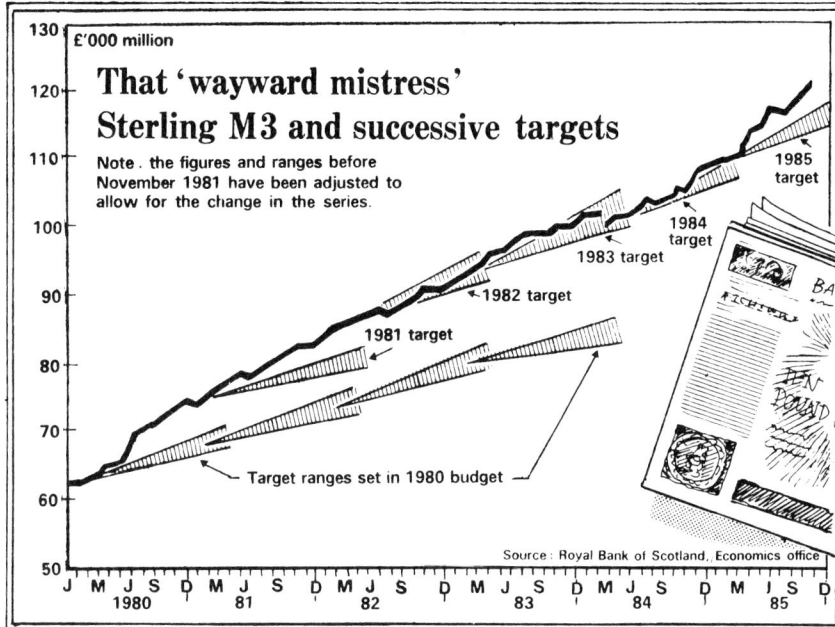

That 'wayward mistress'
Sterling M3 and successive targets

Note. the figures and ranges before November 1981 have been adjusted to allow for the change in the series.

£'000 million

1985 target
1984 target
1983 target
1982 target
1981 target

Target ranges set in 1980 budget

Source: Royal Bank of Scotland, Economics office

Source: *The Guardian* October 24 1985

ACTIVITY 11

A Write a report on monetary policy saying whether it is the best way to regulate the economy.
In your report you might consider the following questions:
- What might have been the costs of monetary policy? – (Use evidence from task 3 and 4.)
- What have been the benefits of monetary policy? (Use evidence from task 3 and 4.)
- Have the benefits exceeded the costs?
- What other information would be needed to decide?
- What alternative policies could have been used to control the economy – (Use evidence from other chapters.)
- Has monetary policy allowed the best use of resources?
- What does best mean?

B Look back at your answers in task 1. Using the knowledge gained in this section, attempt activity 1, questions A and B again.

6.44

Monetary Targets and Actual Outturns

Date announced	Period	Aggregate	Target[a]	Outturn[a]
March 1977	April 1977–April 1978	£M3	9–13	16.0
April 1978	April 1978–April 1979	£M3	8–12	10.9
November 1978	October 1978–October 1979	£M3	8–12	13.3
June 1979	June 1979–April 1980	£M3	7–11	10.3
November 1979	June 1979–October 1980	£M3	7–11	17.8
March 1980	February 1980–April 1981	£M3	7–11	22.2
March 1981	February 1981–April 1982	£M3	6–10	13.5
March 1982	February 1982–April 1983	M1	8–12	12.1
		£M3	8–12	10.9
		PSL2	8–12	10.8
March 1983	February 1983–April 1984	M1	7–11	13.5
		£M3	7–11	9.5
		PSL2	7–11	13.2
March 1984	February 1984–April 1985	M0	4–8	—
		£M3	6–10	12.2
	February 1985–April 1986	£M3	5–9	16.6

Note: (a) Percentage growth at an annual rate, seasonally adjusted

Source: Adapted from *Economic Review* September 1984

Questions in Activity 11 adapted from 'Towards Economic Literacy' *Economic Affairs* 1984 S. Hodkinson and L. Thomas

SECTION 7   Inflation

| HYPOTHESIS | Inflation is a major problem which originates from many sources and requires many cures. |

There is considerable debate among economists concerning the causes of inflation and its solution. They can generally be divided into two groups. Those who adhere to the views of John Maynard Keynes argue inflation can be caused either by excess demand or increasing production costs. Monetarists believe inflation is caused by a more rapid increase in the money supply relative to an increase in output. This debate is outlined in data 7.1 and 7.2.

7.1

'Keynesians have always acknowledged that when demand expands it leads to rises in prices.'

Source: Maurice Peston from *Money Talks* Edited by A. Horrox and G. McCredie Thames Methuen London 1983

7.2

'Inflation is caused by one thing only – a more rapid increase in the quantity of money than output.'

Source: Milton Friedman from *Money Talks* Edited by A. Horrox and G. McCredie Thames Methuen London 1983

TASK 1   To understand the significance and limitations of the Retail Price Index.

Inflation is a dynamic process involving the general price level of goods and services moving upwards over a period of time. This does not mean that all prices are rising but on average the cost of living is increasing. Economists often refer to a fall in the rate of inflation from, for example, 10 per cent to 5 per cent. This does not mean that prices are falling but rather that they are increasing at a lower rate. The inflation rate is measured by the Retail Price Index (RPI), which shows the movement in prices of a basket of goods selected annually by the Family Expenditure Survey. The RPI indicates the change in cost of living as measured by the rate of change of prices for households with a typical consumption pattern. Data 7.3 illustrates the RPI.

7.3

THE STRUCTURE OF THE RPI 1987

A guide to the retail price index

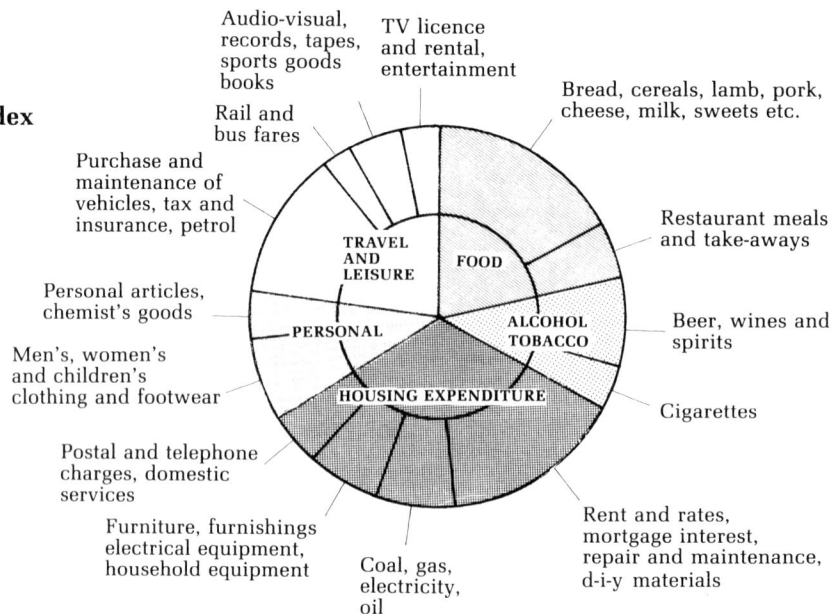

Audio-visual, records, tapes, sports goods books

TV licence and rental, entertainment

Bread, cereals, lamb, pork, cheese, milk, sweets etc.

Rail and bus fares

Purchase and maintenance of vehicles, tax and insurance, petrol

Restaurant meals and take-aways

Personal articles, chemist's goods

Beer, wines and spirits

Men's, women's and children's clothing and footwear

Cigarettes

Postal and telephone charges, domestic services

Rent and rates, mortgage interest, repair and maintenance, d-i-y materials

Furniture, furnishings electrical equipment, household equipment

Coal, gas, electricity, oil

TRAVEL AND LEISURE   FOOD   PERSONAL   ALCOHOL TOBACCO   HOUSING EXPENDITURE

ACTIVITY 1
Examine data 7.4.

A List two main problems of the RPI.

B Why is the RPI important to the government?

C Select a basket of goods which would typify your own consumption pattern and indicate through the use of weights the order of importance of individual items. How far does the official RPI differ from your own consumption pattern? Explain the difference.

D Why did the IFS study suggest that the RPI overstates the increase in the cost of living?

E If the quality of good changes, how might this affect the measurement of changes in the cost of living?

F What particular problems are encountered in the use of the RPI as an accurate measure of the change in the cost of living of lower income groups?

THE COST OF LIVING AS MEASURED BY THE RPI

The Retail Price Index has been criticised in a recent report from the Institute of Fiscal Studies because whilst it generally overstates price rises, it also underplays their effect on the poor.

The RPI is very important to the government because it determines the value of state pensions and social security benefits as well as personal tax allowances and index-linked national savings. All of these and other components of government spending are automatically increased in line with rises in the RPI.

The report concludes that for many years the RPI has exaggerated the rate of inflation and thus government spending has been unnecessarily high. One explanation for this phenomenon is that the weights used in the calculations of the RPI reflect the quantities of goods and services bought in the year preceding the newly calculated index. As a result the index does not accurately reflect current spending habits, so that if the price of one product increases and people purchase a substitute at a lower price, it may be up to two years before the new data is reflected in the index. For this reason the inflation rate is overestimated.

Another criticism of the RPI made by the IFS is that it disregards improvements in the quality of goods. 'Price increases are not fully inflationary if higher prices reflect improved quality.'

Whilst in general terms the RPI overstates the rate of inflation, for low income earners the RPI may understate their 'personal inflation rates'. If, for example, the prices of goods which are heavily purchased by the poor go up disproportionately, such as coal and electricity, the poor will be faced by higher prices than the rich. The IFS calculates between 1974 and 1982 the bottom 10 per cent of households faced price increases on average 8 per cent above those that the richest 10 per cent faced.

Benefits which are indexed linked to the RPI and earmarked for the poor will in fact imply a reduction in their real value.

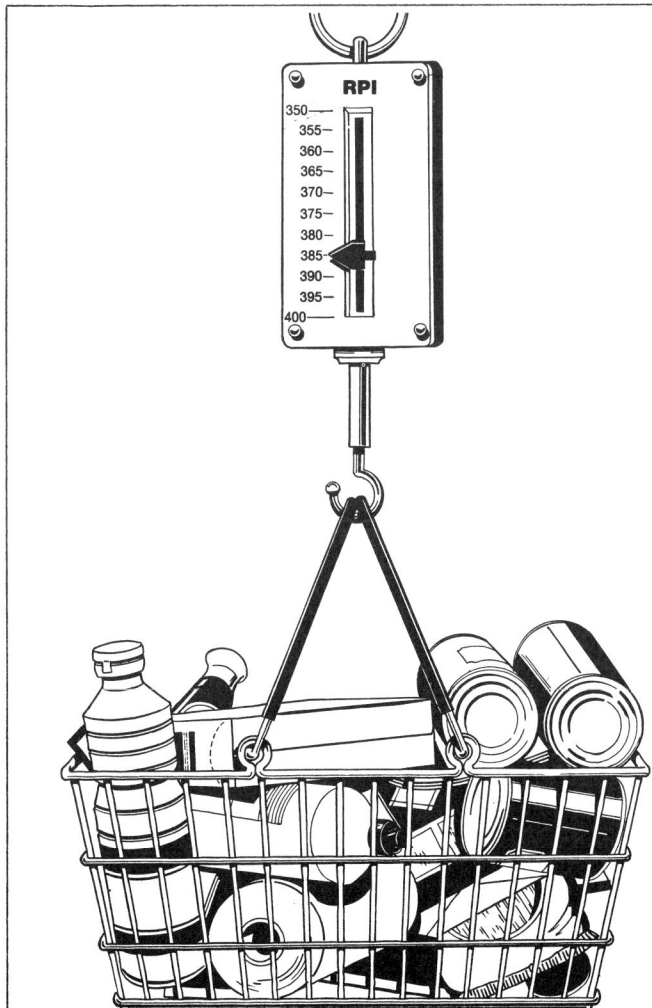

Items included in the Retail Price Index

	Weights, 1989
Food	154
Alcoholic drink	83
Tobacco	36
Housing	175
Fuel and light	54
Durable household goods	71
Household services	41
Clothing and footwear	73
Transport and vehicles	128
Leisure goods	47
Leisure services	29
Catering	49
Fares and other travel services	23
Personal goods and services	37
Total	1000

Source: *Monthly Digest of Statistics* CSO

Source: Adapted from article by Joanna Slaughter The *Observer* May 18 1986 and updated 1989

TASK 2 To discover the problems of inflation.

Inflation is 'public enemy number one' in the minds of many politicians and their advisers.

ACTIVITY 1

In the early 1920s Germany suffered a 'great inflation'. Her money supply increased (if measured by currency in circulation, ie notes and coins) as shown in data 7.5.

Write out in numbers, the money supply in November 1923. By what percentage did the currency inflate between October 1923 and November 1923?

7.5

The Great Inflation

		(marks)
1913	6,000	millions
1914	8,703	millions
1915	10,050	millions
1916	12,315	millions
1917	18,458	millions
1918	33,106	millions
1919	50,173	millions
1920	81,628	millions
1921	122,963	millions
1922	1,295	milliards
October 1923	2.5	trillion
November 1923	92.0	trillion

1 milliard = 1000 millions
1 trillion = A million million million

Source: The Great Inflation W. Guthman and P. Meehan Saxon House Farnborough 1975

ACTIVITY 2

Price increases often move roughly in proportion to changes in the money supply.

With reference to data 7.6, write a paragraph explaining why being a 'millionaire' (in marks) in Germany in November 1923 would not mean that you were wealthy.

7.6

Examples of price changes in Germany

Item Quantity	Pre-War Price	Price in Summer '23	Price in November '23
1 egg	8 pfennig	5000 marks	80 milliard
1 kg butter	2.70 marks	26,000 marks	6000 milliard
1 kg beef	1.75 marks	18,800 marks	5600 milliard

Source: The Great Inflation W. Guthman and P. Meehan Farnborough 1975

ACTIVITY 3

Money has four main functions:
Examine data 7.7.

If there was a hyperinflation such as that experienced by Germany in 1923, how would it affect each of the functions of money?

7.7

A Measure of value – property can be valued in monetary terms, eg 'my motor bike is worth £550'.

2 Store of wealth – one way of storing wealth is to buy a Renoir. Another way is to hoard money in a safe.

3 Standard for deferred payments – if a payment is deferred to a later date payment will be agreed in monetary units.

4 Medium of exchange – money acts as an 'oil to the economy' helping exchange of goods and services to occur.

ACTIVITY 4
Read the extracts in data 7.8 and answer the questions that follow.

A In one year prices as measured by the RPI increase by 10 per cent for fuel and light and 25 per cent for transport and vehicles largely because of increases in oil prices whilst other prices remain more or less constant.

What effect would this have on the two couples? Who would be worse off? Who would be better off?

Explain your answers.

B If the government wanted to protect pensioners from the effects of inflation, can you think of a better means of doing this than simply 'index linking' pensions to the RPI?

C Supposing all items in the RPI went up by an equal amount except for alcohol, which went up by 200 per cent because the government imposed massive taxes on it to try and reduce alcoholism. Would Clive and Frances necessarily have a higher personal inflation rate than Sheila and Charles? Explain your answer.

7.8

Sheila and Charles are pensioners who live in Lincoln on a state pension of £72 a week. This pension is index linked, that is the government increases the pension in line with the inflation rate as measured by RPI. Sheila and Charles spend a high proportion of their income on fuel and light and because they like to visit their grandchildren, who live in London, they spend a lot of money on transport and vehicles.

Clive and Frances are a young married couple who are both employed in managerial posts in a large public limited company. Their joint income is £42,000 per annum and they are able to save a substantial amount of their income. However, they enjoy eating out in restaurants and because they are highly sociable, they spend a substantial proportion of their income on alcoholic drink and meals bought and consumed outside the home.

ACTIVITY 5
Examine data 7.9 and answer the following questions.

A To obtain stable wage rates, what level of unemployment must be accepted?

B If the rate of change of money wage-rates is 10 per cent and the government judges this to be inflationary, from the diagram, suggest what the government might do to reduce money wages?

7.9

The Phillips curve, named after its originator Professor A.W. Phillips, shows the relationship between money wage rates and the level of employment. This relationship was examined in the UK from 1816 to 1957 and the findings plotted onto a graph.

The Phillips curve.

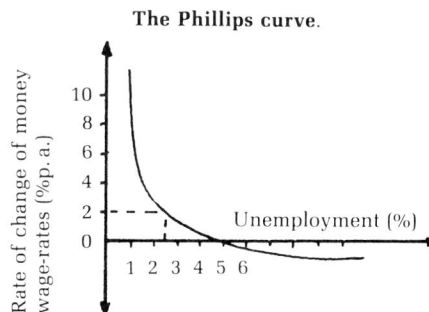

TASK 3   To discover the causes of inflation.

ACTIVITY 1

A   Using data 7.10 to help you, identify a firm's main costs of production.

Study the information in data 7.11–7.13. Answer the following questions.

B   Define, in your own words, what you think is meant by the term 'unit labour costs'.

C   Explain the significance of productivity and expectations in containing the costs of producers.

D   What do you think the economic term 'wage-price spiral' means?

7.10

Source: Ford Motor Company Limited

7.11
Unit labour costs
Productivity rises in the UK continue to make a major contribution to the containment of unit labour costs. Sharp increases in productivity occurred in 1981, 1982 and 1983, with only the miners' strike and a slowdown in the decline in employment moderating the rise in 1984. These increases in productivity have been very important, for pay settlements have not always pointed to a lowering of the inflation rate, with the average earnings index lying significantly above the retail price index in 1983 and 1984. Unit wage costs rose by only 2 per cent in 1983, although the figure is likely to be closer to 5 per cent in 1984. The prospects for inflation may rest upon the capacity of the economy to secure further rises in productivity in the face of a potentially more aggressive round of wage bargaining.

Source: *British Economy Survey* Vol 14 No 2 Spring 1985

7.12
Wage determination and inflationary expectations
Much emphasis has been placed by the government on the reduction of inflationary expectations. Whether one believes this has been achieved by the effect of announcing the strict monetary targets or by the actual experience of rapidly rising unemployment, the reduction in expectations has been considerable. Despite the effects that a falling exchange rate may have on final goods prices, all forecasts see the maintenance of single-figure inflation for 1983. One of the most interesting results has been the willingness of workers to accept longer-term deals (extending beyond the normal 12 month settlement period).

Public sector pay – a thorn in the flesh of many counter-inflationary policies of the past – has also been restrained, with the government adopting a stubborn approach supported by guidelines on public sector pay within a framework of cash limits.

Source: *British Economy Survey* Spring 1985

ACTIVITY 2
Examine data 7.13 and answer the following questions.

A Explain why inflation is expected to fall.

B Briefly explain why the article mentions a strong pound as being significant to the costs of British producers.

C What do you think would be the effect on inflation in the UK of an agreement by oil producing countries, and in particular OPEC, ie a cartel of oil producing exporting countries, to increase the price of oil?

7.13
Fall in costs for industry points to 4% inflation
By Janet Bush
THE GOVERNMENT's prediction that inflation will end the year below 4 per cent was lent support by figures yesterday. These showed a fall in the prices manufacturing industry paid for its raw materials and fuel last month and stable factory gate prices for manufacturers' products.

The Department of Trade and Industry said its index of fuel and raw materials costs fell by 0.2 per cent in May, compared with a rise of 0.4 per cent in April.

In the year to May input prices increased by 1.7 per cent, compared with 1.4 per cent in the 12 months to April.

The drop in the month-on-month figure reflected the strength of the pound against other leading currencies and weaker energy prices.

Source: The *Financial Times* May 1 1987

7.14
Tighter money is needed

Most of the economic indicators show that demand is growing too
fast relative to Britain's ability to produce more. Imports, house
prices, average earnings and inflationary expectations are moving
upwards and the government prediction of lower inflation is not
expected to occur.

The main reason for the over-expansion of demand is loose
money. In March Sterling M3 rose by 1.3 per cent which is too high
a start to a year when it is targeted to rise by 6–10 per cent. In the last
six months Sterling M3 grew by an annual rate of 9.6 per cent.
Although there has been a fall in the velocity of circulation of money
its growth is still too high.

The excessive growth in money has been caused by a massive
expansion in bank lending to the private sector, which rose by £8.1
billion in the last six months compared with £5.5 billion in the
previous six months.

Source: Adapted from *The Economist* April 28 1984

7.15
Demand pull inflation exists when aggregate demand exceeds
aggregate output at, or near, the full employment level. However
it is possible to have simultaneously, excess demand and large
amounts of spare capacity in the economy.

Aggregate demand is simply total expenditure in the economy as
measured by consumption and government expenditure plus
investment, ie the accumulation of capital goods, plus exports
minus imports ie $AD = C + I + G + X - M$. If demand is above its
full employment level an inflationary gap is said to exist.

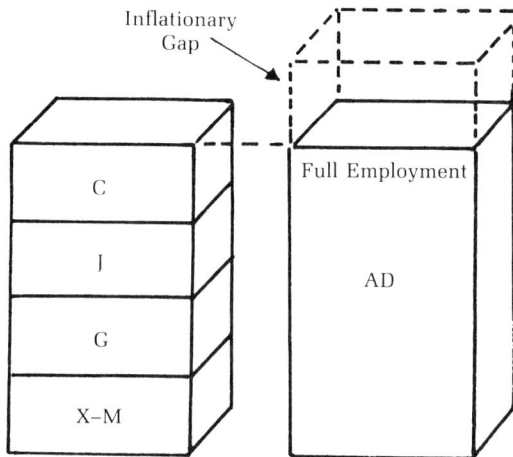

Source: *St. Louis Globe Democrat* 1977

ACTIVITY 4

With reference to data 7.16 and 7.17 answer the following questions.

A   Why, and how, might an increase in the money supply lead to an increase in prices?

B   Why do monetarists tend to suggest that inflation is solely a monetary phenomenon?

Who is to blame for inflation?

7.17

The cause of inflation is said to originate from many different sources. Greedy businessmen, aggressive trade unions, high spending consumers, low productivity and Arab Sheiks raising the price of oil.

Milton Friedman suggests that unions are not the cause of persistent inflation, because in countries such as Japan and Brazil where union power is weak inflation has still been high. OPEC may have imposed heavy costs on the world. However it did not cause lasting inflation, eg in the five years after the 1973 oil shock inflation in both Germany and Japan declined, in Germany from about 7 per cent a year to less than 3 per cent and in Japan from over 30 per cent to less than 5 per cent. In the United States inflation peaked a year after the oil shock. The evidence shows that businessmen are no more greedy in high as opposed to low inflation countries, that inflation can occur in both communist as well as consumer driven capitalist economies and inflation has been extremely high in countries such as Brazil, even though these countries have experienced some of the highest growth rates in the world.

Friedman maintains that the statistical evidence does not support the idea that inflation has many long-run causes but rather that there is only one cause of persistent inflation which is the money supply growing at a faster rate than the rate of increase in output. This is the only common factor which can be identified within countries which have experienced lasting inflation.

Friedman points out that it is the monetary authorities that are responsible for the control of money supply and therefore it is with them that the blame for inflation must rest.

Source: Adapted from *Free to Choose* Milton and Rose Friedman Penguin Harmondsworth 1979

The simple truth

7.16

FIVE SIMPLE TRUTHS embody most of what we know about inflation:

1. Inflation is a monetary phenomenon arising from a more rapid increase in the quantity of money than in output (though, of course, the reasons for the increase in money may be various).
2. In today's world the government determines – or can determine – the quantity of money.
3. There is only one cure for inflation: a slower rate of increase in the quantity of money.
4. It takes time – measured in years, not months – for inflation to develop; it takes time for inflation to be cured.
5. Unpleasant side effects of the cure are unavoidable.

The Monetarist's views are embodied in the old quantity theory of money as represented by the Irving Fisher equation:

$$MV = PT$$

where M = money supply
V = velocity of circulation of money, ie how many times money changes hands
P = average price level
T = number of transactions or output in the economy

The equation is a truism which means that both sides of the equation are representing the same thing but in a different way, ie money multiplied by its velocity must by definition be equal to the average price level multiplied by output because both represent total expenditure in the economy. Monetarists believe that the velocity of circulation of money (V) is stable and therefore conclude any excess growth in the money supply (M) relative to a change in output (T) will lead to an increase in prices (P) in order for the equation to balance.

Source: Adapted from *Free to Choose* Milton and Rose Friedman Penguin Harmondsworth 1980

ACTIVITY 5

Examine data 7.18.

A Outline why inflation was expected to rise.

B Briefly explain what you think economists might mean by the term 'multicausal inflation'.

C What factors would you take into account if you were asked to predict the rate of inflation in the UK over the next twelve months?

7.18

Philip Stephens on the Chancellor's task of convincing the markets

WHY INFLATION FEARS ARE REAPPEARING

The central pledge in the Conservative's election manifesto was that the government would not be content until Britain had stable prices and inflation had been completely eradicated. London's financial markets have still to be convinced it can be done.

Worries about inflation have resurfaced after the general election. The first worry is the rate of earnings growth, which has been running at an annual 7½ per cent and within the last few weeks, has shown some signs of accelerating.

The government's economic strategy assumes that high wage awards will translate over the medium-term into falling employment rather than higher inflation – a tight monetary policy will ensure that producers cannot pass on higher wage costs to consumers.

In manufacturing, the impact of earnings growth on unit wage costs has been offset substantially by productivity gains. Underlying growth in manufacturing productivity is running at between 4 and 4½ per cent a year, but because of favourable cyclical factors the increase since the start of 1986 has been over 6 per cent.

That has pushed down the annual increase in unit wage costs to about 1 per cent.

Productivity growth in the much larger services sector, however, is considerably weaker, while earnings are rising only fractionally less fast than in manufacturing. So, for the economy as a whole, productivity gains average only about 2½ per cent a year, leaving a "core" rate of labour cost inflation of perhaps 4½ per cent.

The second warning signal comes from the buoyant rate of monetary growth in the economy. The broad money-supply measure, M3, once the centrepiece of official policy but now abandoned by the Treasury as a target, has been expanding by nearly 20 per cent a year, while bank credit has been increasing by £2.5bn a month.

House prices, another classic indicator of a potential inflationary build-up, have also been rising sharply.

Third, the international environment is no longer as favourable to the process of disinflation. Oil prices have stabilised and might edge higher, the fall in most commodity prices appears to have levelled off, and inflation in other industrialised nations is on a gently rising trend.

The arguments, however, are not all on one side.

Monitoring of private-sector pay settlements by both the Confederation of British Industry and the Treasury suggests that if anything they are now running slightly below last years's levels – at perhaps 5 rather than 6 per cent. Buoyant earnings growth may thus reflect overtime payments rather than a general upturn in wages pressure.

A recent analysis by James Capel, the City securities house, argues that worries that the economy is in danger of 'over-heating' because of capacity constraints and skill shortages are exaggerated.

The experience of the past few years also suggests that financial innovation and liberalisation have made the links between monetary growth and future inflation more tenuous than ever. The build-up of liquidity in the economy would be a risk in the event of an external inflationary shock – a sudden fall in the value of the pound, for example – but does not necessarily represent a danger in itself.

Moreover, if the international environment is not as favourable, as hitherto, the sluggish pace of growth in most other industrialised countries suggests that the threat of much faster imported inflation is small.

Overall, the conclusion might be – provided the government does not relax its anti-inflation policy – that the task of holding inflation at close to, or a little above, present levels should not be insuperable.

What is much harder to see is a significant stride over the next two years towards the goal of stable prices.

Source: The *Financial Times* June 29 1987

ACTIVITY 6

Much of the monetarists' evidence about the causes of inflation is based upon statistical studies which show a relationship between changes in the money supply and changes in the level of prices. However there are various problems in using statistical studies as proof of economic assertions.

1 Defining what measure of money to use.

2 Effective control of the money supply.

3 Deciding if a relationship between money and inflation implies causation.

4 Distortion of statistics.

A Using data 7.19 and 7.20, examine the argument that the government has not effectively controlled the money supply and therefore other factors may have reduced inflation.

B Using data 7.21, explain what happened to government policy from 1980 to 1987.

7.19

Year	Unemployment (000's)	Inflation Rate (percentage)
75	823	24.2
76	1265	16.5
77	1359	15.9
78	1343	8.3
79	1296	13.4
80	1665	18.1
81	2520	11.9
82	2917	18.7
83	3105	4.6
84	3160	5.0
85	3271	5.5
86	3297	3.4

Source: *Developments in Economics*
Edited by G.B.J. Atkinson
Causeway Press Ormskirk 1987

Source: *Economic Trends* CSO

7.21

There seems to be considerable agreement that £M3 best suits the present circumstances of the United Kingdom. It is well under-stood in the markets. It indicates links with the other policies . . . . It is also relatively easy to define in terms of the banking system.

Source: *Monetary Control* HM Treasury and the Bank of England A Consultation Paper March 1980 pp 3–4

'For broad money (£M3) . . . it is probably wiser to eschew an explicit target altogether .'

Source: Nigel Lawson Budget Speech March 17 1987

7.20

£M3 Targets and Out-turns

Target Period	Target Range	Out-turn	Overshoot from Target Mid-Point
4.75– 4.77	9–13%	17.7%	+ 6.7%
4.77– 4.78	9–13%	16.0%	+ 5.0%
4.78– 4.79	8–12%	10.9%	+ 0.9%
10.78–10.79	8–12%	13.3%	+ 3.3%
6.79– 4.80	7–11%	10.3%	+ 1.3%
6.79–10.80	7–11%	17.8%	+ 8.8%
2.80– 4.81	7–11%	18.5%	+ 9.5%
2.81– 4.82	6–10%	14.5%	+ 6.5%
2.82– 4.83	8–12%	11.0%	+ 1.0%
2.83– 4.84	7–11%	9.7%	+ 0.7%
2.84– 4.85	6–10%	12.2%	+ 4.2%
2.85– 4.86	5– 9%	16.6%	+ 9.6%
2.86– 4.87	11–15%	19.0%	+ 6.0%

Source: 'Financial Statement and Budget Reports'; *Bank of England Quarterly Bulletin*

TASK 4 To identify the main policies that can be adopted by the government to cure the various types of inflation.

ACTIVITY 1

In order to be able to cure inflation the government must diagnose its cause. If the cause is thought to be cost push, then the appropriate cure might be a 'wage policy' to reduce labour costs or a reduction in VAT to cut producer's costs.

Examine data 7.22 and answer the following questions.

A Why does the author anticipate the Chancellor of the Exchequer will take 'counter-inflationary measures'?

B From reading the article what can you infer is the main cause of inflation?

C If the government succeeds in imposing a 'pay restraint', ie an incomes policy limiting increases in income to a level below what they would otherwise have been, would wage earners necessarily be worse off? Explain your answer.

D In your own words explain what is meant in the final paragraph.

7.22

Inflation in Britain running at over 30 per cent

Inflation in Britain has now surpassed 30 per cent and is likely to accelerate further in the next two or three months. At this rate prices double and money and monetary assets lose half their value every $2\frac{3}{4}$ years. It is now hardly conceivable that the Chancellor will delay announcing new counter-inflationary measures involving pay restraint and spending curbs beyond the Summer.

It compares poorly with annual rates for the six months to March in other countries, 8.3 per cent in the United States; 11.8 per cent in France; 7 per cent in West Germany; 10.9 per cent in Japan, 11.5 per cent in Sweden; and 7 per cent in Switzerland. Only Turkey of the 24 industrial countries in the OECD has a rate of inflation near Britain's.

While it would be misleading to express as an annual rate the increase in April alone (it would be 57 per cent), the rise in the first six months of this year will clearly be formidable.

Source: Peter Jay *The Times* May 17 1975

ACTIVITY 2

Incomes policies have frequently been used in post-war Britain to combat inflation. Sometimes this cure is coupled with a prices policy, which gives the government legal powers to restrict price increases. Incomes policies have not had a very good press in recent years and invariably they have been abandoned in the run-up to an election. Using data 7.23 and 7.24 to support your arguments, explain whether you feel the criticisms of incomes policies are justified.

7.23
Criticisms of incomes policy

1 In practice only agreed short-term policies have worked.
2 Certain groups of workers argue they are a special case.
3 Wage differentials become eroded and some workers feel aggrieved.
4 Employers can quite easily evade an incomes policy guideline especially with executives by promoting them in name only and justifying a big pay increase in this way.
5 Private sector workers, especially those who are self-employed can often reduce the effects of a pay policy and this is unfair on public sector workers.

7.24

Years	Type of policy	Result
1947–50	Incomes policy	Collapsed
1961–63	Pay pause	Abandoned
1965–68	Voluntary policy	Relaxed
1971–73	Statutory incomes policy	Confrontation with the miners
1975–78	Social contract	Winter of discontent
1981–	Pay norms and cash limits on public sector pay	Labour shortages in some occupations. Loosely adhered to

ACTIVITY 3

Monetarists argue that the cause of inflation is 'a more rapid increase in the quantity of money than output'. It follows that if the diagnosis is correct, then the cure for inflation is to slow down the rate of increase of the money supply and in so doing the rate of inflation will fall.

Study 7.25 and explain in one paragraph of about 50 words why you agree or disagree with Friedman's views concerning:
● cutting government spending.
● absolving trade unions from causing inflation.
● the danger to democracy in Britain.

7.25

FRIEDMAN HOPE OF 'BETTER CHANCE' FOR BRITAIN

Professor Milton Friedman, this year's winner of the Nobel Prize for Economics who has predicted that Britain has only a 50 per cent chance of preserving democracy because of the country's economic problems, last night said he might revise his prediction after what he saw as a change in government policy.

Professor Friedman said he had been heartened by the speech made by Mr Callaghan to the Labour Party Conference.

In his speech Mr Callaghan gave a warning of the dangers of continuing to spend more than we earn. The belief in the need to cut government spending formed one plank of a three-point prescription for national recovery put forward by Professor Friedman.

He (Friedman) said trades unions could not be blamed for causing inflation by demanding high wage increases. This was only a symptom of inflation which had been caused by a lack of monetary control and the government spending more than 50 per cent of national income.

High inflation led to polarization between sections of the community which would lead to a breakdown of democracy if left unchecked.

Source: *The Times* November 10 1976

ACTIVITY 4

Examine data 2.26.

Assume aggregate demand in the economy exceeds output at full employment, and as a result there is inflation. If you were an economic adviser to the Shadow Chancellor of the Exchequer advise him of the appropriate cure to this economic problem. Be sure to warn him of the potential pitfalls of applying the cures you advocate.

Demand pull inflation has been a rare phenomenon in the United Kingdom in recent years. Lord Keynes explained how the government could manage demand to rid the economy of this type of inflation. In essence, the government must take measures to reduce the level of demand. It could, for example, reduce consumer spending by raising taxes and therefore cutting down on disposable income that individuals receive. The effect of this would be to reduce the 'inflationary gap' and thereby reduce inflation.

The problem of managing demand in the way advocated by Keynesian economists is that it is very difficult to be precise about the effect of tax or interest rate changes. As a result, it is quite possible that aggregate demand may be reduced by too much and thus there might be deficient demand leading to unemployment. Some economists advocate constant 'fine tuning' of the economy in order to try and prevent such problems occurring.

7.26

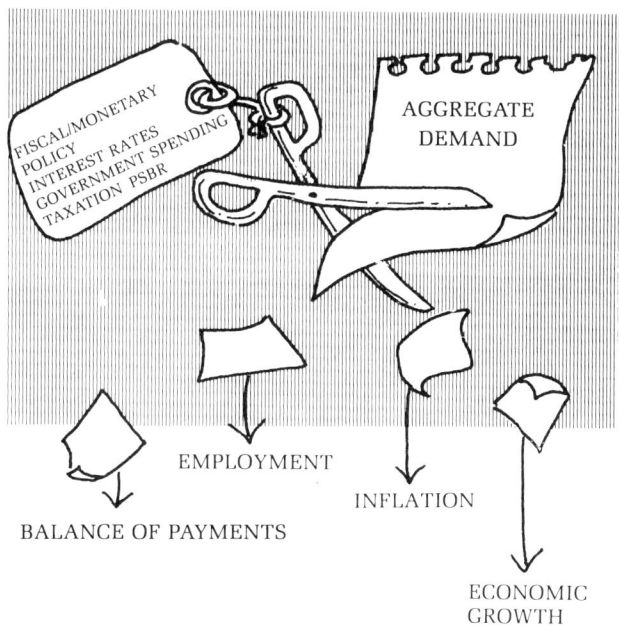

TASK 5 To examine government policy since 1970 and to identify the reasons for the various policies that were implemented.

ACTIVITY 1

A Examine data 7.27 and explain why inflation grew to such high levels in 1975 and 1978.

B Why did inflation at first rise, and then fall, after the Conservative government came to power in 1979?

7.27

Government policy and economic events

1971–72	Chancellor Barber's dash for growth ie tax cuts and public expenditure increases.
1971–73	Edward Heath's statutory incomes policy.
1973–74	OPEC quadruple the price of oil.
1971–74	Money supply grew by 92 per cent.
1973–75	Inflationary expectations of workers and employers are high, resulting in high wage demands and expected high price increases.
1975	Labour government under pressure from the IMF cut government expenditure, introduce social contract, ie prices and incomes policy, and set monetary targets that lasted until the winter of 1978.
1979–86	Conservative government introduces its Medium–Term Financial Strategy (MTFS), which involves cutting the size of the PSBR (mainly via cuts in public expenditure) as a proportion of national income in order to control the money supply and therefore control inflation.
1978–79	OPEC raise the price of oil.
1979	Exchange rate of sterling rises significantly due to high interest rates in the UK and the exploration of North Sea oil.

ACTIVITY 2

Using data 7.28 do you think the Labour government of 1975–79 was monetarist or Keynesian? Explain your answer.

7.28

'We used to think that you could spend your way out of a recession and increase employment by cutting taxes and boosting government spending. I tell you in all candour that that option no longer exists, and that in so far as it ever did exist it worked by injecting bigger doses of inflation into the economy followed by higher levels of unemployment as the next step ... that is the history of the past twenty years'.

Source: Extract from a speech made by James Callaghan at the Labour Party Conference September 28 1976

ACTIVITY 3

In the light of the newspaper headlines in data 7.29 and Mr Lawson's quote in data 7.21, do you think the Conservative government of 1987 is monetarist or Keynesian? Explain your answer.

7.29

The Economist

JANUARY 4 1986

The year monetarism dies?

Is monetarism working?
'The policies are not working'
by Andrew Britton

Why Milton's monetarism is bunk

Oxford Dons show why Friedman is 'devoid of empirical support'

Friday October 18 1985

Monetarism is dead—official

SECTION 8   The Balance of Payments

HYPOTHESIS	The balance of payments will present major problems for the UK when North Sea oil runs out.

Many political commentators suspect that Harold Wilson lost the 1970 UK election to Edward Heath because of the announcement of a deficit in the monthly balance of payments figures a few days before polling day. Although still an important economic variable, it has taken back stage over the last ten years with the rate of inflation, the unemployment level and rate of exchange moving to the fore. This has been largely due to the support given to the accounts by North Sea oil. However, many feel that this economic variable will assume increasing importance as the production of domestic oil runs down. Others feel that the British economy has altered significantly since 1979 and will be strong enough to pay its way in the world without the oil. These differences of opinion are reflected in the quotations in data 8.1–8.3. Which of the quotes in data 8.1–8.3 reflect the view that the UK will have problems when North Sea oil runs out?

8.1

'The bounty of the North Sea oil will remove the constraint on growth for some years to come. It will also disguise, however, not only any growing price uncompetitiveness but also, and more important, the basic structural weakness of our economy.'

Source: A.P. Thirlwall February 1978 *National Westminster Quarterly Bank Review*

8.2

'The committee concluded that the contraction in the UK manufacturing sector and the trade deficit associated with it "constitute a grave threat to the standard of living of the nation".'

Source: House of Lords Select Committee quoted in *Lloyds Bank Economic Bulletin* November 1985

8.3

'This report needs to be set in perspective if we are not to get a totally biased and misleading view of the performance and prospects of our economy.'

Source: Leon Brittan referring to a report of the House of Lords Select Committee 1985

TASK 1   To understand the structure of the UK balance of payments account.

ACTIVITY 1

A 'A country cannot spend more than it earns.' To what extent is this statement reflected in the definition of the balance of payments in data 8.4?

8.5

Visible Trade – trade in goods, eg cars.
Invisible Trade – trade in services, eg tourism.

8.4
WHAT IS THE BALANCE OF PAYMENTS?
A country's balance of payments accounts are a statement of its residents' transactions with residents of other countries. They are in two parts: the current and capital accounts. The current account is a measure of how much residents are receiving from abroad through sales of goods and services (exports) compared to how much they are spending on goods and services produced by overseas residents (imports). The capital account, on the other hand, records inflows and outflows of capital in the form of loans, investments and bank deposits. There is no reason why either the current or the capital accounts, when considered in isolation, should balance, but the way that the balance of payments accounts are drawn up ensures that capital account transactions, in total, offset current account transactions – hence the name 'balance of payments'.

Source: *A Guide to the International Financial System* Banking Information Service

ACTIVITY 2

Study the figures in data 8.6

A What trend can you identify in the visible balance?

B What singular fact is noticeable about the invisible balance?

C Are there any worrying signs in the overall current account between 1978 and 1985?

8.6

UK Balance of Payments

£ million

	1978	1979	1980	1981	1982	1983	1984	1985
Current account								
Visible trade								
Exports (fob)	35 063	40 687	47 422	50 977	55 565	60 776	70 367	78 051
Imports (fob)	36 605	44 136	46 061	47 617	53 234	61 611	74 751	80 162
Visible balance	– 1 542	– 3 449	1 361	3 360	2 331	– 835	– 4 384	– 2 111
Invisibles								
Credits	24 848	33 224	41 008	56 635	64 592	65 224	76 737	80 608
Debits	22 341	30 492	39 440	53 836	62 986	61 255	71 141	74 895
Invisibles balance	2 507	2 732	1 568	2 799	1 606	3 969	5 596	5 713
Current balance*	965	– 717	2 929	6 159	3 937	3 134	1 212	3 602

*Current balance = visible balance + / – invisible balance

Source: CSO

ACTIVITY 3

Examine data 8.7

A What was the visible balance in 1980? Why was it particularly worrying that this had increased to – £4384 million by 1984?

B What is invariably the biggest item in invisible exports?

C When an English person enjoys a holiday in Greece is this considered an export or import in the UK balance of payments? Why?

D According to the information in data 8.8, what factors have been tending to cause a deficit and a surplus on current account?

E What two factors suggested in data 8.8 have led to the growing interest, profits and dividends?

8.7

£ million

	1980	1981	1982	1983	1984	1985
Credits						
Exports (fob)	47 422	50 977	55 565	60 776	70 367	78 051
Services:						
General government	317	407	407	473	474	490
Private sector and public corporations						
Sea transport	3 816	3 784	3 267	3 054	3 254	3 272
Civil aviation	2 210	2 359	2 471	2 665	2 931	3 188
Travel	2 961	2 970	3 188	4 003	4 614	5 451
Financial and other services	6 371	7 364	8 162	9 428	10 110	11 852
Interest, profits and dividends						
General government	943	948	816	616	606	554
Private sector and public corporations	22 590	36 189	42 990	41 449	50 950	52 478
Transfers						
General government	958	1 658	2 157	2 221	2 370	1 812
Private sector	842	956	1 134	1 315	1 428	1 511
Total invisbles	41 008	56 635	64 592	65 224	76 737	80 608
Total credits	88 430	107 612	120 157	126 000	147 104	158 659
Debits						
Imports (fob)	46 061	47 617	53 234	61 611	74 751	80 162

Source: CSO

8.8

In the late 1970s the North Sea oil bonanza provided an increasing visibles' surplus, which reached its maximum in 1981. Since then there has been a steep decline in the manufacturing sector, which has been matched to a certain extent by a steady rise in invisibles.

In another respect, too, the invisibles appear to be coming to our aid. After the abolition of exchange controls in 1979, investment funds were able to seek higher profits abroad. With the decline in the value of the pound since then these foreign investments have grown in sterling value and are now producing interest, profits and dividends (invisible earnings) at such a rate, that they nearly managed to make up for the rapid decline in the oil surplus resulting from the 50 per cent fall in the price of oil in 1985–86.

Source: *British Economy Survey*

I'm only here for the beer

ACTIVITY 4

A In 1985 UK residents spent £4,877 million on foreign travel. Consult data 8.7. Did we enjoy a surplus or deficit on travel?

B Consult data 8.9 and 8.10.
What are the attractions of holidays on islands like Corfu? What factors will determine the extent to which expenditure on foreign holidays increases in the future? Try to incorporate the concept of income elasticity of demand in your answer.

8.10

Income elasticity of demand

$$= \frac{percentage\ change\ in\ demand}{percentage\ change\ in\ income.}$$

A low income elasticity shows a smaller relative percentage change in demand in response to a change in income.

A high income elasticity shows a greater relative percentage change in demand in response to a change in income.

8.9

'An old favourite with timeless pleasures'

The enchanting island of Corfu attracts more British visitors annually than all the other Greek islands put together. For it has a special magic all of its own. Abundantly green and fertile, it's an incredibly beautiful place. It offers an astonishing variety of scenery: from pine-clad mountains to gentler hillsides, terraced with ancient olives folding round lush valleys of corn and citrus groves. The horizon is picked out by the spires of tall slender cypresses which form a stunning backdrop to the indelibly blue sea. Around the coastline are marvellous beaches, and hundreds of sheltered inlets and coves.

Source: *Simply Greece* Thomson Summer 1987

ACTIVITY 5

A What is meant by a deficit?

B What explanations are given in data 8.11 for the large trade deficit?

C What effects did the figures have on other economic indicators?

8.11

Trade balance moves heavily into red

The Department of Trade and Industry announced yesterday that the UK had a balance of trade deficit for May of £1,161 million.

Allowing for a surplus on invisibles of £600 million, the current account was in the red by £561 million.

A statement from the Treasury suggested that the figures were due to the UK's exceptionally high rate of economic growth compared to our trading partners. Certainly there was a rise in the demand for capital goods and semi-manufactured goods as well as things like cars, washing machines and videos.

However, confidence in the City was affected. The price of shares fell, particularly those of blue chip companies. The value of the pound remained fairly firm against the dollar.

Source: Adapted from an article by Anne Segall The *Daily Telegraph* July 23 1987

ACTIVITY 6
Study data 8.12 carefully.

A   The visible balance in 1974 was £5.4 billion. What was the invisible balance?

B   There was a current account deficit of £3.3 billion in 1974. This was balanced by the inflow of investment and borrowing. The borrowing in effect meant that the UK could add £0.1 billion to reserves and finance the current account deficit. Errors and omissions reduced the deficit by £0.1 billion. Following the above, how was the £6.5 billion current account surplus of 1981 balanced?

The Capital Account
The table shows how the balance of payments balances eg how in 1974 the current account deficit of £3.3 billion is financed. A distinction is drawn between 'official financing', ie transactions concerned with the management of the official reserves – and all other investment and other capital transactions.

Investment and Other Capital Transactions
There are 2 main categories:–

1   **Portfolio investment**: the purchase of foreign securities.

2   **Direct investment**: investment in productive capital assets such as factories and plant and machinery.

8.12
Summary of the UK's Balance of Payments in 1974 and 1981

	1974 (£ billion)	1981 (£ billion)
Current Account Balance	– 3.3	6.5
Capital Account Investment and other capital transactions (inflow +; outflow –)	1.6	– 7.4
Official Financing ●.Net foreign currency borrowing (increase +; repayment –)	1.7	– 1.7
● Movements in reserves (additions to –; drawings on +)	– 0.1	2.4
	1.6	0.7
Balancing Item	0.1	0.2
Capital Account Balance	3.3	– 6.5

Source: *United Kingdom Balance of Payments* 1983 Edition

Official Financing
This includes the government's investment and borrowing transactions which are concerned directly with the management of the official reserves.

The Balancing Item
This reflects errors and omissions in the trade statistics and ensures that the current and capital accounts sum to zero. The figures for official financing are exact, but most other entries in the balance of payments accounts are estimates.

ACTIVITY 7
Consider data 8.13 which represents the latest presentation of balance of payments introduced in 1987.

A   Compare the new presentation with the original. What are the main differences?

B   Give two examples of items in the account which are not found in this presentation and can now only be found in the subsidiary accounts. Refer to data 8.12 to help you.

C   Does the balance of payments balance each year?

8.13
UK Balance of Payments

	1986	1st qt	2nd qt	3rd qt	4th qt
		(£ million, not seasonally adjusted)			
Current balance	– 1,100	+ 176	– 507	– 1,119	+ 350
UK external assets and liabilities					
Transactions in assets	– 86,946	– 14,721	– 14,291	– 41,011	– 16,941
Transactions in liabilities	+ 81,206	+ 13,546	+ 11,903	+ 42,019	+ 13,738
Net transactions	– 5,758	– 1,175	– 2,388	+ 1,008	– 3,203
Balancing item	+ 6,858	+ 999	+ 2,895	+ 111	+ 2,853

As students of the balance of payments will quickly realize, the new presentation is at once simpler and less informative. There is less data to help understand movements in other economic variables, though admittedly most of the statistics previously available can be elicited from subsidiary tables. However, it is certainly simpler in that it emphasizes the current balance, which is the catalyst of the whole account, and downgrades the private investment flows.

Source: *British Economic Survey* Spring 1987

ACTIVITY 8

Consider Victor Keegan's article.

A Explain how a pre-electoral boom may have caused the poor trade figures for May.

B What sort of foreign goods do you think UK citizens tend to buy when extra income is gained from tax cuts?

C Distinguish between what Keegan would consider the long-term and the short-term factors which would determine the balance of payments.

The conspiracy theory?

8.14

The trade figures announced yesterday would appear to support what Mr. Roy Hattersley was saying during the election campaign. He felt that tax cuts and easy credit generating a 'consumer boom', would lead to a balance of payments crisis. It is conceivable that the near record monthly current account deficit of £561 million was the result of a boom electoral victory. The UK economy has major weaknesses threatening its long-term growth, but these are not the immediate cause of the May deficit. The Chancellor could correct the present problem by deflating the economy, perhaps by raising interest rates.

The fundamental problem of the economy is highlighted by the large deficit in manufactured goods. Britain's long-term propensity to import more than it exports has accelerated with revenue from North Sea oil. In 1986 we imported £5.4 billion more manufactured goods than we exported. This is not a problem which can be cured overnight.

Source: Adapted from an article by Victor Keegan in *The Guardian* July 23 1987

TASK 2 To investigate the effects of North Sea oil on the UK balance of payments.

While trade in manufactured goods has moved into deficit, the production of North Sea oil has kept the balance of payments position healthy. The crucial question is whether the British economy can become more competitive and maintain a sound balance of payments position, when the oil is exhausted.

ACTIVITY 1

Consider data 8.15. Then attempt the following questions.

A Describe the trends, and anticipated trends in the consumption and production of oil between 1976 and 1990.

B When did the UK become self-sufficient in oil?

C What implications has the chart for the UK balance of payments?

8.15

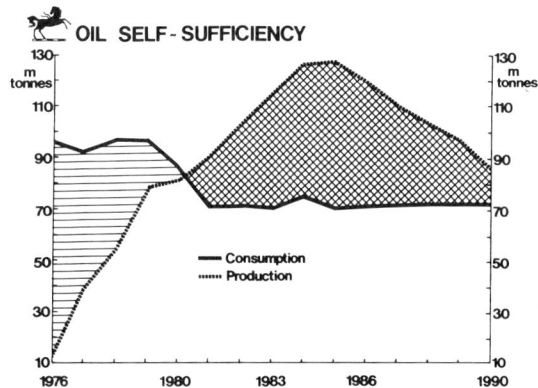

OIL SELF-SUFFICIENCY

— Consumption
······ Production

Source: *Lloyds Bank Economic Bulletin* September 1985

ACTIVITY 2

A Using the statistics in data 8.16, draw a graph plotting the course of the four balances (invisible, oil, current account and non-oil visible) between 1984 and 1993.

B What conclusions can you draw from the graph?

8.16

Table 1
THE DECADE AHEAD: SOME ARITHMETIC

	Net oil exports (crude) m tonnes	Oil trade balance £bn	Non-oil visible balance £bn	Invisible balance £bn	Current account balance £bn	% gdp
1984	52	7.1	−11.2	5.2	1.1	0.3
1985	52	8.0	−11.0	5.5	2.5	0.7
1986	48	6.7	−12.1	6.1	0.7	0.2
1987	40	5.6	−13.3	6.7	−1.0	0.2
1988	32	4.5	−14.6	7.3	−2.8	0.6
1989	25	3.5	−16.1	8.1	−4.5	1.0
1990	17	2.4	−17.7	8.9	−6.4	1.3
1991	11	1.5	−19.5	9.7	−8.3	1.5
1992	4	0.6	−21.4	10.7	−10.1	1.7
1993	−1	−0.1	−23.6	11.8	−11.9	1.9

Notes: 1984, actual. 1985, estimated from first three quarters. 1986-1993, projected on following assumptions. Oil production falls at 6.2% p.a, oil consumption rises at 1.4% p.a, oil price £140/tonne. Non-oil and invisible balances increase at 10% p.a, nominal gdp at 7.5% p.a. Oil products trade is in balance.

Source: *Lloyds Bank Economic Bulletin* January 1986

TASK 3   To evaluate the importance of manufacturing and services to the UK balance of payments.

The task invites you to consider the reasons for the decline in manufacturing and whether a growth in services can compensate for this decline.

ACTIVITY 1
Examine data 8.17 carefully.

A   Listed below are a number of reasons for the decline in UK manufacturing. Decide for yourself, or perhaps in a group, those reasons which you feel have caused the decline in manufacturing, and those which have resulted from it.

Explain your answers.

Reasons for decline in manufacturing include:
- a rigid class structure
- an education system which lends too little prestige to the engineer
- trade unions
- the economic policy of Mrs Thatcher
- the effect of North Sea oil on the exchange rate
- lack of investment
- poor management
- no industrial policy to match that of W. Germany, France or Japan
- joining the EEC

B   Having re-read the article, explain what you consider would be the implications for the UK economy in the next decade.

How serious a problem

8.17

The seriousness of the problem may be illustrated by some key facts about manufactured products, related to exports and our share of world trade; to imports; to manufacturing output in Britain; and to productivity and competitiveness.

Britain's share of world trade in manufactured goods has declined steadily throughout this century, with some short pick-ups. The actual volume of exports of manufactured goods has risen substantially in the last twelve years (with some decline in 1975 and 1980 to 83), and in 1985 reached a record level. Our share of world trade had, however, fallen to 7.6 per cent by 1984 – from 14.2 per cent in 1964 and 20.5 per cent in 1954. Happily, in 1985, our share recovered a little to about 8 per cent, but exports of manufactured goods in the first five months of 1986 were lower than in the first five months of 1985.

Imports of manufactured goods into Britain have risen in the last twenty years by much more than our exports. Our exports as a percentage of imports had fallen from 220 per cent in 1963 to under 100 per cent in 1983, and have moved lower since. There was a very sharp rise in the volume of imports in 1975–79 and in 1981–85. They have continued to increase in 1986 compared with the early part of 1985.

Hence the balance of trade in manufactured goods has changed from a surplus of between £1½ billion and £6 billion in each year from 1963 to 1982, to a deficit in 1983, which widened to nearly £4 billion in 1984, with only a small improvement in 1985, small despite a splendid export achievement. Reasons for anxiety are not confined to the global figures. It is clear that trade in more 'modern' products (such as electronics) is in deficit as well as the 'traditional' even 'declining' groups. And the deficit is mainly attributable to the very large imports of capital and consumer manufactured goods. Lack of competitiveness has led to a sizeable reduction in Britain's manufacturing base; and the consequent reduction in capacity has made it easier for importers.

Between 1960 and 1983 in our manufacturing industry

output rose by	26 per cent
exports rose by	130 per cent
imports rose by	500 per cent

Source: *The Royal Bank of Scotland Review*

ACTIVITY 2

As the colour supplement advertisements indicate, there is continuing use of technological invention in the manufacture of motor cars. Conduct a survey into the country of origin of the car owned by parents of your colleagues.

Put your findings in the form of a pie chart and calculate the import penetration percentage.

You can do this by calculating

$$\frac{\text{the number of foreign cars}}{\text{total numbers of cars}} \times 100$$

What reasons do people give for buying foreign cars?

8.18

VORSPRUNG DURCH TECHNIK.

THE FACES in the room dropped in unison. Audi's aerodynamics expert, Dr Burkhardt Leie, broke the stony silence in the politest possible way.

'IT'S NOT fashion, it's not chic. It's a major re-evaluation of aerodynamic values.'

THE REAR of the new Audi 90 looked as though it wouldn't be out of place on a race circuit.

'VERY FASHIONABLE, very chic', we ventured.

Source: Audi

8.19

RENAULT 5 GTX

With a 1721 cc engine, this luxurious model can cruise Autobahns at 100 mph with a top speed of 115 mph, and includes tinted glass, halogen headlamps, electric front windows and central door locking with infra red remote control as standard, all from only £7,130 (3-door version).

Source: Renault UK

ACTIVITY 3

A Describe the trends taking place in data 8.20 and 8.21.

B What conclusions can be drawn from this data?

8.20

Trade performance of UK manufacturing industries 1975–85

	Trade balance 1985 £ billion	Exports/imports 1975 percentages	1985	Imports/home demand 1975 percentages	1985	Exports/sales 1975 percentages	1985
High research intensity							
Chemicals and allied products	2,366	150	134	23	38	32	46
Office and data-processing machinery	− 670	107	84	73	102	71	102
Electronic and electrical engineering	− 1,261	128	84	23	46	30	41
Motor vehicles	− 2,978	199	58	24	52	39	38
Aerospace equipment	1,016	176	136	28	64	42	72
Instruments engineering	− 290	111	85	51	62	54	57
TOTAL	− 1,787	**150**	**94**	**29**	**54**	**37**	**52**

Source: *Midland Bank Review* Autumn 1986

8.21

UK/EEC trade by product

	1973 £ million	1982 £ million	Per cent of total 1982 deficit	Percentage change over the period
Road vehicles	− 93	− 2.200	44	2.265
Textiles	− 27	− 600	12	2.122
Iron and steel	− 73	− 500	10	585
Plastics	− 62	− 400	8	545
Footwear and clothing	+ 29	− 250	5	962

Note: Total UK manufacturing goods deficit with EEC in 1982 was £4.98 billion.
Source: Overseas Trade Statistics HMSO

Source: *National Westminster Bank Quarterly Review* February 1986

ACTIVITY 4

Read the short extracts in data 8.22. These suggest that the UK's poor trade performance in high research intensity industries has been governed in part by the policies of multinational companies.

A   Why are multinational companies necessary in some lines of production?

B   What criteria do such companies have for investing in one country rather than another?

High research intensity industries   8.22

In the pursuit of global production and marketing strategies, decisions by multinational companies can have a marked impact on the trading position of individual countries. The worsening of the UK's motor vehicle trade performance during the past ten years is partly a consequence of decisions taken by Ford and General Motors to supply a greater proportion of the market from production plants in Belgium, West Germany and Spain. The production of motor vehicles and aircraft on a competitive basis in the UK is now only possible through international collaboration. In all but the most sophisticated product areas, the competitive position of the UK's high research intensity industries has been eroded, particularly by products from Japan and newly-industrialised countries in the Far East.

The impact of giant companies
In many industries, especially those involving high levels of research and development (R & D), there are undoubted advantages in being one of the largest producers. Since the end of the Second World War, large companies have tended to become more important in industrialised economies. The growth of markets, coupled with the expansion and liberalisation of international trade, and the increasing complexity of many products, have enabled large companies to reduce unit costs through scale economies of mass production and R & D. In many product areas, the costs of developing new technologies are such that only the largest companies are able to compete in the world market. Huge resources are necessary to sustain long-term investment programmes which may not begin to yield a return for anything up to a decade after the products have been launched. Large companies are also in a position to spend the sums necessary to ensure that their new product ranges are flexible, so that alterations can be made in response to changes in consumer taste and the general trend towards shorter product life cycles. Although new technologies and products are often developed by small companies, it is difficult for them to exploit the market in the long term against competition from large MNEs with established access to worldwide markets and huge resources for promotion and further product development. Larger companies are also in a better position to cater for national differences in taste and styling.

Source *Midland Bank Review* Autumn 1986

ACTIVITY 5

Explain in a short paragraph, using your own words, why 'conventional trade figures have become a nonsensical way to describe the real state of business relations between countries'. Use data 8.23 to help you.

An inside job in Japan   8.23

Japanese consumers spend three times as much each on foreign-brand goods as American consumers do on the goods of Japanese firms. This is a teaser with which Mr Peter Drucker, a business guru, likes to confound those who say Japanese markets are closed to foreign goods. Why, then, does Japan have a $96 billion trade surplus, of which $51 billion is with America?

The answer lies in the success that foreign companies – such as Nestlé, Coca-Cola, NCR and IBM – have in producing their goods in Japan and selling them there, rather than exporting them to Japan. This business does not show up in the trade figures that hit the headlines each month to anger American and European politicans. But it is big – more than three times as big as Japan's trade surplus. It is also relatively profitable: as a percentage of their sales, the operating profits of Japanese affiliates of foreign companies are about one-third higher than the operating profits of Japanese companies.

Source: Adapted from *The Economist* 11–17 April 1987

8.24

ACTIVITY 6

Data 8.24 would seem to suggest that the UK's anticipated deficit in trade in unlikely to be matched by a growth in services.

A Which services are our main earners of foreign currency? Why do you think services in general are more difficult to export than manufactures?

B What reasons are given for believing that manufacturing is essential to our trading position?

Table 2

UK EXPORTS IN 1984

	£bn	% of total	% of imports
Food, beverages and tobacco	4.7	5	57
Basic materials	2.0	2	41
Oil, fuels, lubricants	15.4	17	157
Semi-manufactures	18.3	20	99
Finished manufactures	28.3	31	89
Other	1.7	2	276
Total visible exports	70.4	77	94
Sea transport	3.2	3	74
Civil aviation	3.0	3	118
Travel	4.2	5	90
Financial	2.8	3	n.a.
Consultancy	1.2	1	n.a.
Students, diplomats, bases	1.6	2	n.a.
Other services	4.8	5	n.a.
Government services	0.5	1	34
Total services exports	21.3	23	123
Total exports	91.7	100	100

Source: *UK Balance of Payments* 1985

Prospects for services exports are not particularly good, even though the UK relies more heavily on services for its export revenue than do other industrial countries. The UK's share of world services trade fell slightly faster than its share of world manufacturing trade between 1968 and 1983 from 11.9 to 7.3 as opposed to from 9.6 to 6.2 per cent. The volume of services exports rose by only $\frac{1}{2}$ per cent a year in the decade to 1984, while that of goods other than oil rose by about 2 per cent. Table 2 gives the relative importance of different kinds of export. Apart from oil, civil aviation and some of the other services show the best coverage of imports by exports, while food, raw materials and sea transport have the worst. Financial services, although they have a high export margin, yield no more than 3 per cent of total export revenue. Semi-manufactures are in balance; it is finished manufactures which have an unfavourable ratio of only 89 per cent coverage of exports by imports.

Source: *Lloyds Bank Economic Bulletin* January 1986

ACTIVITY 7

Nigel Lawson remained confident even in the face of the massive deficit of August 1987. This he blamed on the importation of 'E' registered motor cars, ie a freak month. Examine data 8.25.

A Explain how an improvement in the productivity of manufacturing could improve the balance of payments.

B How might a depreciation of the pound improve the balance of payments?

8.25

PRODUCTIVITY, THE POUND, AND UK EXPORTS

Nigel Lawson, the Chancellor of the Exchequer is optimistic about trade in manufactures. He feels that the improvement in the UK's productivity (output per man) will reduce the price of our manufactures, making them more competitive at home and abroad. It is also possible that as the oil runs out the pound will depreciate on the foreign exchange – less pounds will be demanded to buy it.

This will make our exports cheaper. Consider the following example:

Exchange rate £1: $2.00.
A UK motor car priced at £5,000.
This car will be priced at $10,000 in USA.
If the exchange rate for the pound were to depreciate to £1: $1.50 then the car would be priced at $7,500 in USA.
This improved competitiveness may improve our trading position.

N.B. This is a very simplified account and there are several reasons why it would not work out like this in practice.

TASK 4 To investigate why the balance of payments position acted as a constraint on the rate of growth of the British economy in the 60s and 70s, and to consider whether it will soon re-emerge as a constraint as the oil gradually runs out.

ACTIVITY 1

Study data 8.26.

A Explain what was meant by stop-go.

B Why did the policy of stop-go weaken the long-term competitiveness of Britain? (Make sure you understand the part played by investment in this analysis.)

8.26

This procedure, instead of alleviating the trade and payments difficulties faced by Britain after the war – out-of-date capacity, loss of empire, huge debts – added further difficulties by eroding the competitive position of British manufacturing. The slow-down in demand and in investment reduced the rate of productivity growth. Therefore, when the economy was reflated, British industry was less competitive than it had been before the crisis, imports rose more rapidly than before and so precipitated the next crisis. The policy designed to correct the immediate balance of payments problem helped create the longer-term deterioration of the balance of payments position.

Of vital importance, however, were not so much the fluctuations in demand, the stops and the goes, as the low general rate of growth of demand. Britain's balance of payments position could not sustain an average rate of growth demand as great as that enjoyed by her competitors. In particular, the rate of growth of demand for manufactures was significantly lower in Britain than in other major industrial countries.

Stop-go

This was the era of stop-go – of recurrent balance of payments crises, each more severe than the one before. The response to each crisis made sure of that.

The reaction of successive governments to balance of payments crises was to deflate the economy by tax increases and restrictions on credit, and by limiting the spending power of wage earners by means of incomes policies. The old policy of discouraging investment at times of balance of payments crises was also continued. The overall strategy undoubtedly worked. Imports were cut, and some sort of balance was restored to the balance of payments. When balance was restored, the economy was boosted again, usually by the politically popular expedient of cutting personal taxes to encourage consumption.

Source: *Whatever happened to Britain* John Eatwell Duckworth/BBC London 1982

ACTIVITY 2

Study of data 8.28 allows us to carry the analysis a little bit further. The UK is shown to have a high income elasticity of demand for finished manufactures. You will remember from task 1, activity 4 that this means that people have a greater relative change in demand to a change in income, ie they buy proportionately more finished goods as their income rises.

A If incomes rose by 5 per cent in both the UK and W. Germany, by what percentage would the demand for finished manufactures rise in each country? Use the formula in data 8.10 to help you.

B Using the cartoon, give a list of the kind of manufactures which are imported when incomes rise.

C How do the figures help to explain the stop-go phenomenon?

8.27

8.28

Income Elasticities of Demand for Imports

	UK	W Germany	France
Food, beverages and tobacco	0·35	0·86	0·84
Basic materials	0·66	1·22	0·70
Fuels	2·47	2·66	1·26
Manufactured goods	3·09	2·14	2·19
semi-manufactures	2·37	2·06	na
finished products	4·30	3·52	na
Total imports	1·82	1·31	1·63

na = not available

Source: *Lloyds Bank Review*

ACTIVITY 3

Predictions about the state of the economy in 1995 may be well wide of the mark. Jeremiahs may be confounded by new discoveries of oil, a transformation in manufacturing or better than expected returns from overseas investment. Optimists may be disappointed by a failure of industry to respond to reduced taxation, lower exchange rates and diminished union power. William Keegan has long been a critic of Mrs Thatcher's overall economic strategy. Study data 8.29.

A Why should one not pay too much attention to one month's statistics?

B On what does he blame the weakness of the UK's balance of payments?

C Compare and contrast Jock Bruce-Gardyne's views in data 8.30 with those of Keegan.

8.29

Now, one of the important rules in the interpretation of economic statistics is that one should not pay too much attention to one month's figures. It is quite possible that the June statistics will not be so bad. But the trend and its implications are unmistakeable. From now on the contribution of North Sea oil will fall. The poisoned chalice of the first two Thatcher/Howe/Lawson economic stewardships has reached their own lips. Those who were suspicious of the recent boom have been proved right.

And at some time we shall have to witness an almighty exchange rate crisis in order to get the balance of payments in shape once more.

Source: William Keegan The *Observer* July 26 1987

8.30

Optimists dismiss most of this as scare-mongering, a classic example of the national propensity to discount the possibility of success. Unlike the Barber boom this one is for real. Notwithstanding one month's trade return – reflecting statistics distorted by industrial disruption in the Civil Service – the evidence from industry is that our share of markets both at home and overseas is recovering at last. Thanks to surging output our unit costs are now growing more slowly than those of our principal competitors. Instances of capacity restraints on increased production are in fact exceptions, not the rule.

Source: Jock Bruce-Gardyne The *Daily Telegraph* July 23 1987

ACTIVITY 4

A The balance of payments deficit of August 1987 confirmed the views of some that the supply side factors had not worked. Try to explain how supply side policies could improve the balance of payments.

B The news in September 1987 that Britain's manufacturing output had at last regained the level of 1979 may show that the UK has turned the corner. How does the hypothetical scenario in data 8.33 highlight the importance of manufacturing recovery for the UK balance of payments?

8.31

The school of thought that the underlying character of the economy has been transformed by a supply side-led boom is not now so convincing because we appear to be watching a re-run of a good old British problem, in which growth is gradually curtailed by the balance of payments.

Source: Hamish McRae The *Guardian* September 1987

8.33

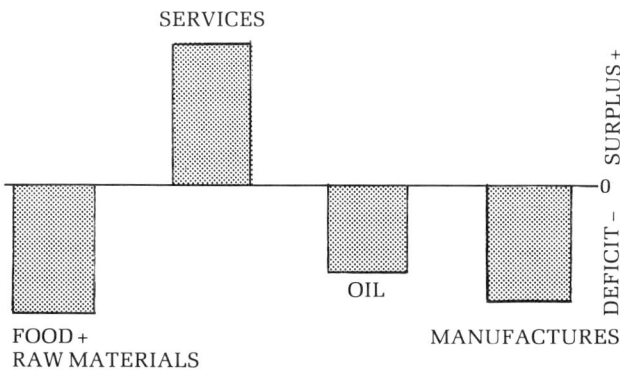

8.32

The supply side-led boom school of thought believes it is necessary to create an environment in which the private sector will flourish. Mrs Thatcher is closely allied to this belief and strategy of the Conservative party which was reported in the '*Economic Progress Report*' of June 1979 as being... 'based on four principles: first, the strengthening of incentives, particularly through tax cuts, allowing people to keep more of their earnings in their own hands, so that hard work, ability and success are rewarded; second, greater freedom of choice by reducing the State's role and enlarging that of the individual; third, the reduction of the borrowing requirement of the public sector to a level which leaves room for the rest of the economy to prosper; and fourth through firm monetary and fiscal discipline, bringing inflation under control and ensuring those taking part in collective bargaining are obliged to live with the consequences of their actions'.

SECTION 9 International Trade

| HYPOTHESIS | Free trade gives a greater output of goods and services, and a higher standard of living than trade protection. |

Trade between countries takes place because individual countries are not self-sufficient; although they might like to, they cannot produce all the goods they need themselves. The quotes opposite represent two contrasting views on international trade. In practice, countries may feel it is necessary to protect their industries against foreign competition by giving their goods some form of advantage. Certain economists disagree! This section examines the potential problems and benefits of both free trade and protection.

9.1

'The control of international trade may be the only way of recovering and maintaining prosperity.'

Source: Wynne Godley October 1978

9.2

'It is urgent that the trend towards protection be reversed, and that freer world trade be promoted.'

Communiqué from the IMF Interim Committee meeting. April 17–19 1985

TASK 1 To discover the reasons why, in practice, countries protect their industries against foreign competition.

ACTIVITY 1

A Read through the section from *The Japanese Conspiracy*. Why do you think this is sometimes called the 'infant industry' argument for protection?

B What do you think is meant by the headlines in data 9.4? Why do some MPs hold these views?

C What possible consequences might arise from the attitudes and possible action expressed in data 9.4?

The Japanese Conspiracy

9.3

Over 12 years Japan's exports of hi-tech products have increased more than seven times to $40 billion. In 1970 Japan's balance of payments surplus with the US was $1 billion, by 1980 it had reached $10 and by 1982 $21 billion. Japan's protectionist policy ensures the strength of its industry against competition from abroad while it 'assaults' foreign markets with exports. Before any car is shipped to Japan it is subject to elaborate testing in order to meet the strict requirements.

In the 1950s America and Europe were the main producers of machine tools, with the US producing an estimated $1.8 billion of output. Japan's industry was not in a position to compete at this stage of its development, but by 1980 it accounted for over 50 per cent of the market. Japan initially relied on strict tariffs on US imports and quotas on the number of goods entering the country. Over time, trade liberalised as companies grew and merged to form conglomerates, encouraged by legislation (in 1961 companies that merged were granted tax relief by the government).

Source: Adapted from *The Japanese Conspiracy – A Stunning Analysis of the International Trade War* M. J. Wolf The New English Library London 1984

Snubbed Mrs T plots war

By SIMON WALTERS and JOHN KAY

PREMIER Margaret Thatcher is poised to deliver a karate chop to Japanese imports in a bitter new trade war.

She warned last night that she will hit back hard unless Tokyo ends its dirty-tricks campaign to stop Britain selling in Japan.

Mrs Thatcher spoke in the Commons as MPs from all sides protested at the Japanese double-dealing which has given them a £3.7billion profit from trade between the two countries.

Mrs Thatcher is also furious about a snub from Japanese Prime Minister Yasuhiro Nakasone. She wrote to him on March 4 about the bid by Cable and Wireless for a massive telecommunications contract in Japan.

But she had to tell MPs yesterday that Nakasone has not even bothered to reply.

SLAP THOSE JAPS OVER TRADE, SAY ANGRY MPs

Source: The Sun March 27 1987

HOW THE NIPS DO US DOWN

9.4

THE CHEATING Japanese use a whole box of dirty tricks to keep foreign goods out of their country.

They impose enormous tariffs on imports. And they make up complicated rules and quality-control standards to apply to British goods.

Japan slaps a tax on Scotch whisky **SEVEN TIMES** higher than on their own brands. A bottle of imported Scotch costs £60.

British and other foreign firms are banned from buying stocks in the soon-to-be-privatised Nippon phone company. Yet their financial institutions bought heavily into British Telecom.

Highly-complex testing procedures for all foreign goods can take up to **ONE YEAR** to process.

Drug companies cannot break into Japan because of miles of red tape.

Questionnaires running to 20,000 pages have to be filled in first.

And British farmers cannot sell pork to Japan—even through it is the most popular meat in their diet.

The Nips moan that we import meat from Latin America, where there is foot-and-mouth disease.

Our chocolates are banned on the ridiculous grounds that a special emulsifying agent is not approved by Japan.

But no other country in the world objects to the substance.

ACTIVITY 2

Study data 9.5 which relates to a drug imported from the United States.

A What argument could be suggested in support of protection?

B Which of the methods of protection from data 9.3 would be most suitable to use in this case?

State your reasons.

9.5

'I wish I could get hold of the people who made the drug and . . . make them take the damn tablets themselves'.

Mr Roberts had suffered from arthritis for 25 years before he started taking the drug in 1981. Six months later, he began to experience discomfort and irritation when ever he went into the sun. A string of other disorders also developed: long hair began to appear in patches in unexpected parts of his body, his finger and toe nails grew at a rate much faster than normal, his eyesight deteriorated and he suffered from digestive and bowel trouble.

Rightly or wrongly, he thought these problems were linked to the drug. And, although his doctor didn't agree, he stopped taking it. Even today, his skin still becomes red and blotchy when exposed to sun.

Source: *Which?* February 1987

ACTIVITY 3

Examine data 9.6.

A What reasons for protection are suggested?

B Outline any objections the US had to the Japanese trading policy.

9.6

Cutting rough with Japan's chip makers

The American Department of Commerce has proposed the imposition of countervailing tariffs against Japanese manufacturers of 64K memory chips. It is also investigating complaints that the Japanese are dumping the new, 256K memory chips in the US market. The Japanese now dominate sales of memory chips. They also account for 20 per cent of the entire US semi-conductor market. The Commerce Department argue they have achieved this unfairly and have imposed countervailing duties on chips sold at less than cost price. Although some parts of the industry are healthy, prices in others have fallen greatly. They have been selling recently for as low as $2; the average price of a 256K chip fell from $18–20 to $3½ between 1984 and 1985.

The Americans blame the Japanese for this fall in prices. In an effort to find new markets, given the fall in computer and video sales, Japanese firms such as Hitachi, Toshiba and NEC are flooding America with exports. Pressure to find outlets for their products has increased with the expansion of capacity in their new factories.

The Japanese have reacted to the proposal by raising prices on memory chips sold in America by 20 per cent. NEC and Hitachi have also announced a cut in the production of 256K chips, producing, by March, only 50 per cent of the amount planned.

Source: Adapted from *The Economist* January 11 1986

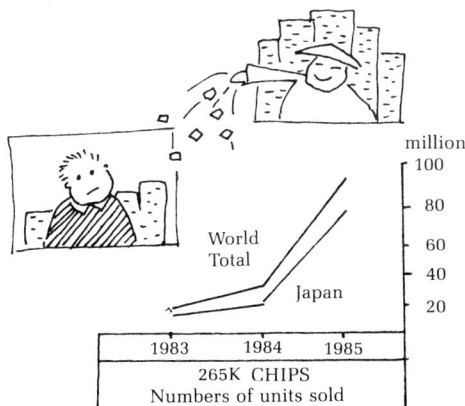

million
100
80
World Total
60
40
Japan
20

1983   1984   1985
265K CHIPS
Numbers of units sold

ACTIVITY 4
Study article 9.7.

The Protection debate is not new. In the early 1970s the US President attempted to use protection measures.

A What is meant by a '10 per cent surcharge on imports'?

B What reasons are given for protection?

9.7

Nixon acts to save dollar

The US President Richard Nixon tonight announced the suspension of the right of countries to convert dollars into gold. This announcement precedes negotiations which will, to all intents and purposes, result in a devaluation of the dollar against other currencies.

The US hope that this will end the speculation and uncertainty concerning the value of the currency and also strengthen its trading position. In addition Mr Nixon announced a 10 per cent surcharge on imports to the United States and a 90 day wage and price freeze to start immediately. This is intended to strengthen the US balance of payments and avoid the possibility of the first deficit since 1893.

The United States indicated that the action was taken in order to make it more competitive in world markets, and because it was unsure if other countries would agree to a revaluation of their currencies against the dollar.

Source: Adapted from articles by Anthony Thomas The Times August 15, 17, 1971

ACTIVITY 5
Examine data 9.8.

A In what way is the British aerospace and motor industry being protected, and for what reason.

B Why may the US object to this protection?

9.8

Billion pound boost to Airbus and Rover

by Ian Williams

INDUSTRY ministers are preparing plans for a pre-election boost to Britain's aerospace and motor industries which will mean the injection of up to £1 billion of public funds.

Geoffrey Pattie, an industry minister, has decided that British Aerospace must get financial support to remain in Airbus Industrie, the European consortium. He also wants to ensure that Britain participates in the development of a new generation of airliners, the A330 and A340.

Industry ministers are also in favour of a sanitised version of the Rover corporate plan, presented to them late last year by the Rover boss Graham Day, involving an increase of equity and loans up to £400m.

BAe has asked the government for £750m of repayable launch aid to develop the new Airbus models which will cost £2.5 billion. They are designed to compete with the American giants, Boeing and McDonnell Douglas.

Pattie confirmed to The Sunday Times last week that it is no longer a case of whether his department will support BAe — merely the best way of putting the package together. "We are taking a positive attitude. We are looking at ways in which it can be done," he said. A support package will be ready for discussion elsewhere in Whitehall by the end of the month.

Earlier this week he angrily dismissed American government trade representatives who had flown into London to take him to task over alleged subsidies to Airbus. Hours after the Americans left, Pattie issued his most forthright statement yet in support of Airbus, a statement that has convinced Sir Raymond Lygo, managing director of BAe, that financial support is certain.

BAe reckons a decision to support the A330 and A340 will create up to 12,000 jobs in its factories.

Meanwhile, Rover, the state-owned car group, moved last week to quash any suggestion that its corporate plan, now being considered by ministers, will contain any shocks — least of all any serious job losses in sensitive Midlands marginal constituencies.

By contrast, before Christmas it had implied that the plan would be the most radical yet, with everything open to scrutiny.

The plan is likely to stress continuity. The disposal of peripheral businesses such as Unipart and Leyland Bus to their managements will be highlighted, and the sale of Istel to its management will follow. The trucks business will go to DAF of Holland or Paccar of America.

There will be no plan to dispose of Land Rover this year, and any structural change in the Austin Rover volume car business, particularly involving closer collaboration with Honda, is likely to be deferred.

The plan will have to talk money, however, with the Rover Group likely to reveal losses of up to £250m for 1986. Ministers may resist giving a full £400m which could infuriate backbenchers alarmed at the £4 billion of government loans and guarantees the company has already swallowed.

At the least, a modest cash injection, some debt write-off and an increase in borrowing limits are likely when the plan is published in a few weeks.

Source: Ian Williams The Sunday Times February/March 1987

ACTIVITY 6
Study data 9.9.

A   Why may Japan feel the need to protect such essential industries as agriculture?

B   What problems may result from this protection?

9.9

Japan's bed of unsavoury rice

The Venice summit next month has agricultural trade as a priority on its agenda. Japan will use this in order to push through reforms of its over protected and inefficient agricultural industry.

Once regarded as an essential provider of decent agricultural incomes and self-sufficiency in food, it has increasingly been criticised for its inefficiency.

Attitudes to the industry are changing. Not only do consumers pay more than eight times the world price for rice but land prices have risen so high that many Japanese living in urban areas are not able to afford their own home. This situation has resulted from the 1 billion Yen in subsidies given to the industry each year.

Despite the change in attitudes, reform will be slow as agricultural reform usually requires changes in the law.

Source: Adapted from *The Economist* April 1987

ACTIVITY 7
Examine the figures in data 9.10.

A   How important are customs duties in raising revenue for the government?

B   If tariffs were placed on the price of imported goods what problems may result in the UK?

Examine data 9.11
C   Why might a country wish to use an *ad valorem* rather than a specific tariff?

9.11

An *ad valorem* tax/tariff – An indirect tax/tariff which is expressed as a proportion of the price of the good.
A specific tax/tariff — An indirect tax/tariff which is expressed as a given absolute sum of money per unit of the good.

9.10

Tax revenues, 1988

	£million
Income tax	43 199
Corporation tax	17 306
Capital gains tax	2 172
Development land tax, inheritance tax and estate duty	1 103
Stamp duties	2 345
Petroleum revenue tax	1 506
Alcohol	4 520
Tobacco	5 021
Betting and gaming	893
Hydrocarbons	8 503
Customs duties	1 644
VAT and car tax	27 952
Rates	18 530
Motor vehicle duties	2 777

Source: *Financial Statistics* HMSO January 1989

ACTIVITY 8
In task 1 you have examined some of the main reasons why individual countries may protect their industries. You should now be able to write a few short sentences, with examples, outlining these reasons. How many of these reasons could be used to justify the protection of UK industry today?

TASK 2   To discover the evidence in favour of, and against trade protection.

ACTIVITY 1
The data represents the arguments of two economic institutions concerning protection.
Read both items carefully.

A   Contrast the views expressed in each article.

B   Examine the OECD report. Which countries and goods do you feel are not included in the report?
Does this invalidate it in your opinion? Give reasons in support of your argument.

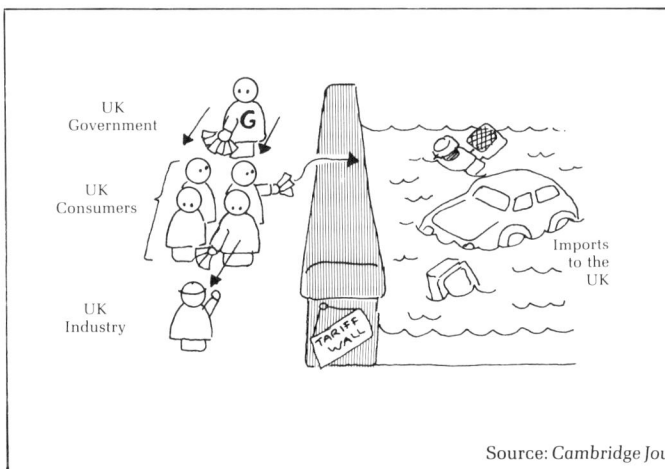

9.12

Control of imports as a means to full employment and the expansion of world trade: the UK's case
Francis Cripps and Wynne Godley
Propositions
(1)   Fiscal expansion accompanied by direct control of imports (whether through tariffs or quotas) is the only practical means by which the UK, and probably several other industrial countries, can sustain expansion of national output sufficient to restore full employment in the next decade.
(2)   The use of import controls with fiscal expansion to raise the level of activity need not be a 'beggar-my-neighbour' policy. The total volume of other countries' trade will not be diminished, provided that there is no retaliation, that the country introducing import controls does not use them to secure a larger trade surplus or smaller deficit than it would otherwise have done, and that the composition of its imports does not shift in favour of 'surplus' countries. Indeed, if the composition of its imports is shifted against 'surplus' countries and the latter do not retaliate, the total volume of world trade will rise, enabling the rest of the world to expand production; 'surplus' countries will regain elsewhere trade which they have lost in the country which discriminates against them and therefore will have no valid reason for retaliation.
(3)   Control of imports need not 'featherbed' inefficiency in domestic industries. On the contrary, expansion of demand made possible by import control is likely to assist innovation and productivity growth.
(4)   Creeping protectionism, adopted on an *ad hoc* basis, may reduce world trade if it is operated mainly against 'weak' suppliers and may perpetuate inefficiency if it involves the subsidy of obsolete processes in conditions of stagnation.

Source: *Cambridge Journal of Economics* 1978

9.13

The Costs and Benefits of Protection.
This report concentrates on import restrictions which affect manufacturers in OECD countries. It evaluates the effect of restrictions on trade, prices, employment and competitiveness. The main findings are:
(1)   Protection has yielded few benefits but high costs. Measures tend to be complex and the effect of their implementation often differs from the intention.
(2)   The effectiveness of demand policies to generate growth can be reduced if governments engage in restrictions and tariffs which drive prices up.
(3)   Protection has not proved effective in sustaining employment. Jobs saved by protection are often as a result of jobs lost elsewhere in the economy.
(4)   Discriminatory restrictions, on certain goods, have limited impact in reducing imports.
(5)   Uncertainty, as a result of restrictions, leads to a fall in investment.

Evidence presented in the report

(1)   Quantitative restrictions, eg quotas, create upward pressure on prices as goods become scarce. The UK clothing industry had an average increase of 20 per cent of retail prices in the period covered. This gives increased revenue to the exporting country.

(2)   Similarly, protection (notably voluntary export restraint) provides large transfers of money to foreign producers – Japanese steel profits from sales to the US market increased by 10 per cent.
(3)   Restrictions often result in trade diversion, one set of suppliers replacing another. From 1976–80 EEC imports from Asian countries increased 2.2 per cent annually, but supply from Mediterranean countries increased 9.5 per cent.
(4)   Protection is only likely to maintain employment in industries with low productivity and little scope for modernisation, eg the clothing industry. Canadian restrictions on apparel imports protected 7.5 per cent of jobs in 1980. In the US automobile industry employment however increased by no more than 22,000 over the period to 1982 from its restriction with Japan, while the recession reduced unemployment by ten times this. Restrictions tend to redistribute rather than generate employment.
(5)   It has been estimated that a 15 point rise in tariffs in OECD countries would cause a significant reduction in growth by 1995, industrial countries would suffer a loss of 3.3 per cent of GDP.

Source: Adapted from: *The Costs and Benefits of Protection* OECD 1985

ACTIVITY 2

Read the article on voluntary export restraint, a new form of protectionism.

A   What evidence is there to suggest the growth of the VER as a method of protection?

B   Compare the use of a VER with a more direct method such as a tariff or a quota (restricting the quantity of goods which are allowed to enter a country). Which method is better for:
   - the Treasury
   - the Retail Price Index
   - the governments of the two countries involved?
   State your reasons in each case.

9.14

Voluntary export restraint

A VER is usually defined as an agreement between two parties whereby one agrees to restrict the volume of its exports to the other 'voluntarily'. One example can be seen in the agreement between the Japanese Automobile Association and the British Society of Motor Manufacturers and Traders, who agreed that the Japanese share of the new car market in the UK should not be greater than 11 per cent in any one year. In addition, agreements have taken place between the UK and a number of other countries, over a variety of goods. The UK currently has agreements with Korea, Poland and Taiwan over footwear and Korea, Taiwan and Japan over music centres. The multi-fibre agreement, which restricts imports of 114 categories of textiles from over 30 countries, operates in a similar way. VERs tend to be between only two countries or industries, although Europe as a group has an agreement with Japan on video-cassette recorders. Restrictions generally apply to one exporting country only, and last for a specific period of time. (A UK restriction for 12 months on Japanese TVs would not for example apply to imports of TVs from other countries.)

Benefits of VERs:
1.   They reduce imports and encourage the development of import substitute industries. There is less pressure to remove them than tariffs and they are easier to review.
2.   Governments are seen to be 'doing something' to prevent imports. Costs are less than tariffs and they do not affect the budget.
3.   Exporting countries would prefer VERs rather than suffer a tariff, and they can raise their prices on other exports to recover revenue.

Operation
1.   Domestic demand for goods slopes from left to right, more goods are bought at lower prices.
2.   Domestic supply slopes from right to left, more is supplied at a higher price.
3.   Without restraint home goods sell at P* where demand = supply.
4.   If world supply is WS1, changes in home demand for imported goods do not affect the world price OP1; OZ goods are bought at price P1.
5.   At price P1 home suppliers will only produce OW. The difference is made up by imports of WZ.
6.   If a VER is negotiated, domestic supply is required to expand to OX, imports must fall to XY. This drives up the domestic price to P2 and so domestic demand falls to OY.

Source: Adapted from 'New Ways of Restricting Imports' *Economic Review* David Greenaway November 1985

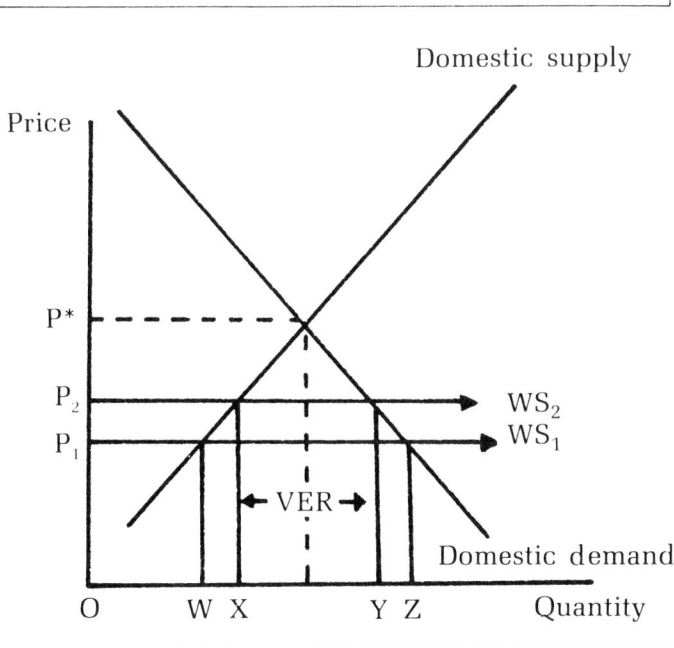

ACTIVITY 3

A   Included in tasks 1 and 2 are a variety of protection measures. List as many as you can, stating which are direct, on goods, and which help industry indirectly.

B   Using your list, decide which measures could apply to the reasons given for protection in task 1.

C   From the data so far, outline the potential benefits and problems of protection.

TASK 3   To discover the ideas behind the arguments for free trade.

Despite the continued use of protection, economists and international trade organisations such as GATT argue strongly that free trade needs to be promoted.

ACTIVITY 1

A   Examine data 9.15–9.17. List any items which are in support of free trade.

B   Look at data 9.18. Is it in favour of free trade or against it? What reason is suggested?

9.15

★ **FIVE international deals without money:**
1   Ford swaps cars for sheepskins in Uruguay.
2   Pierre Cardin is paid in silk for advising the Chinese about fashion.
3   General Motors swaps cars for bauxite in Jamaica.
4   The Philippines swaps coconut products for Romanian machine tools.
5   Malaysia swaps crude oil for iron ore with Brazil.

Source: *Daily Mirror* June 22 1987

9.16

Free trade

In a country which is regarded as having one of the world's more open economies, it is odd that the debate concerning the benefits and problems of free trade should be so heated. This debate is certainly not new. It appears that a free trade pact with the USA will be the best way to ensure the competitiveness of Canada's manufacturing industry and also to maintain its share of imports to America.

Exports now account for 30 per cent of Canada's GNP. Free-traders argue that the market mechanism is required to promote efficient home industry. The C D Howe Institute, an economic 'think tank' in Toronto, presents its case by comparing the growth of GNP per capita of the Canadian and Argentinian economies since the 1920s.

Both countries had almost the same GNP per capita in the 1920s but since 1925 GNP has only grown by 65 per cent in Argentina compared to 265 per cent in Canada. This, they argue, is due to Argentina's protectionist policies.

The stress placed on Canada's competitiveness resulted from the recession of 1981–82. Output stagnated from 1975–82 and the lack of growth in output led to higher wage costs (Canada's were 27 per cent higher than the USA).

Against these potential benefits economic nationalists argue that Canada's industry would suffer from direct competition, and that a small home market and inefficient industry is an acceptable price to pay for political independence.

Source: Adapted from *The Economist* February 15 1986

9.17

"Personally, I can't see that there'll ever be the slightest demand for this stuff in the old country."
Source: *Punch* 1947

9.18

Source: Liberal party poster Weidenfeld and Nicolson

ACTIVITY 2

Read data 9.19–9.21.

It is argued that free trade can benefit all countries. In data 9.19 trade benefits both countries because each has an absolute advantage in one good. This idea first appeared in *The Wealth of Nations* 1776, when Adam Smith showed the way output and efficiency could be increased. What reason is given in data 9.21 for increased efficiency?

9.19

The United Kingdom and New Zealand both produce manufactured goods and food products. The UK however is generally better at making manufactured goods and New Zealand is generally better at food products. They each are relatively more efficient in one good, producing at a lower cost and a higher output. By concentrating on the things they produce best and trading, they each have a greater quantity of goods than if they had tried to be self-sufficient, producing both goods themselves.

9.20

'Countries have an absolute advantage when . . . each country is capable of producing both goods but each of them is more efficient than the other at producing one of the goods.'

Source: *First Economics* G. F. Stanlake Longman Harlow 1986

9.21

A man not educated to this business could scarcely make one pin a day and certainly not twenty. But in the way this trade is carried on it is divided into a number of branches . . . one man draws out the wire, another straights it, a third cuts it, a fourth points it, a fifth grinds it at the top . . . . Each person could make one-tenth of 48,000 pins a day.

Source: *The Wealth of Nations* Adam Smith First published 1776

ACTIVITY 3

Read through data 9.22 completely.

A simple set of figures can be used to illustrate the theory of absolute advantage. An economic model is used with only two countries and two goods to simplify things.

A In which good does country A have an absolute advantage and in which good does country B? Say exactly why. Calculate how much more productive each country is compared to the other.

B Compare the total output after trade to that when countries were self-sufficient.
By how much has each country benefited? In conclusion, if trade has been of benefit it is because each country has an absolute advantage; they are more efficient in producing one good compared to the other country.

9.22

Production possibilities

Each country has 10 units of resources (land, labour, capital and enterprise). Using all resources on one good only:

Country A	Country B
Could make either	Could make either
400 videos	200 videos
or	or
200 hi-fis	400 hi-fis

Self-sufficiency

Each country attempts to make both goods, dividing resources so that 5 units are used in the production of each good.

Country A	Country B	Output
Does make	Does make	300
200 videos	100 videos	videos
and	and	300
100 hi-fis	200 hi-fis	hi-fis

After specialisation

Countries specialise in the good in which they have an absolute advantage, using all 10 resources on that good.

Country A	Country B
400 videos	0 videos
0 hi-fis	400 hi-fis

After trade

Trade takes places at 1 video for 1 hi-fi. If country A trades 150 videos to country B, it gets 150 hi-fis in return. Each country is left with 250 of its original goods.

The reason why countries might trade at 1 video for 1 hi-fi is examined in more detail, in the next activity.

Country A	Country B	Output
250 videos	150 videos	400 videos
150 hi-fis	250 hi-fis	400 hi-fis

ACTIVITY 4

Would trade still be beneficial to both countries if one had an absolute advantage in both goods? David Ricardo's example of trade between the UK and Portugal in cloth and wine (1817) illustrated that trade would still benefit both countries providing they specialise in producing goods in which they have the greatest comparative advantage. Read through data 9.23–9.25 completely. This illustrates a situation where one country has an absolute advantage in both goods.

A Why does country A have an absolute advantage in both goods?
How much more productive is country A in each good than country B?

B To work out which good country A has a comparative advantage in and which good country B has a comparative advantage in:

Method 1.

How much more productive is country A than B in videos? How much more in hi-fis? Country A has the comparative advantage where this figure is greatest. Country B has a comparative advantage (or a least comparative disadvantage) where this figure is smallest.

Method 2.

Use the opportunity cost ratio. Look for the lowest opportunity cost, ie to produce 1 video find out how many hi-fis both countries have to give up. The country with the lowest number of hi-fis given up has the comparative advantage in videos. Work out the comparative advantage in hi-fis by finding the least number of videos given up. You should find the same answer whatever method you use!

C Compare the total output after trade to that when each country was self-sufficient. By how much has each country benefited?

9.23

'Countries have a comparative advantage when . . . one country has a comparative cost advantage over the other. Comparative cost relates to the opportunity cost of producing the commodities.'

Source: *Introductory Economics* G. F. Stanlake Longman Harlow 1986

9.24

Opportunity cost

The value of the alternative forgone to achieve a particular thing.

Source: *Penguin Dictionary of Economics* G. Bannock, R. E. Baxter and R. Rees Penguin Harmondsworth 1979

9.25

Production possibilities
Each country has 10 units of resources (land, labour, capital and enterprise).

Country A	Country B
Could make either	Could make either
400 videos	320 videos
or	or
400 hi-fis	160 hi-fis

Opportunity cost – In country A 1 video for 1 hi-fi, in country B 2 videos for 1 hi-fi or 1 video for $\frac{1}{2}$ hi-fi.

Self-sufficiency
Each country attempts to make both goods, dividing resources so that 5 units are used in the production of each good.

Country A	Country B	Output
Does make	Does make	360
200 videos	160 videos	videos
and	and	280
200 hi-fis	80 hi-fis	hi-fis

After specialisation
Countries specialise in the goods in which they have the greatest comparative advantage. Note in this example country A does not specialise completely; total specialisation would lead to a fall in the output of videos from 360 to 320. In this example country A devotes 2 resources to videos and 8 to hi-fis. (In country A 1 unit of resources will produce 40 videos or 40 hi-fis.)

Country A	Country B
80 videos	320 videos
320 hi-fis	0 hi-fis

After trade
The terms of trade, the rate at which videos exchange for hi-fis, will be between the two internal opportunity cost ratios. Only then will both countries benefit. Let's assume trade takes place at 1 hi-fi for $1\frac{1}{2}$ videos. If country A trades 100 hi-fis it gets 150 videos in return from country B. Country A now has 150 + 80 videos and is left with 220 hi-fis, country B is left with 170 videos.

Country A	Country B	Output
230 videos	170 videos	400
(80 + 150)		videos
220 hi-fis	100 hi-fis	320
		hi-fis

ACTIVITY 5
So far comparative advantage has been explained using opportunity cost. This is the same as comparative cost; by finding the lowest comparative cost it is possible to identify those goods in which countries have a comparative advantage. Examine data 9.26.

A   Which country has an absolute advantage in both goods? Remember in this example it is the lowest cost per unit, not the highest output.

B   Compare the production cost of textiles to the cost of cars in country A. What fraction is it? Now compare the production cost of textiles to cars in country B. The country with the comparative advantage in textiles will have the lowest fraction.

9.26
Comparative costs of cars and textiles
Production cost per unit

	COUNTRY A	COUNTRY B
CARS	£4000	£6000
TONS OF TEXTILES	£100	£200

Source: Overseas Trade Statistics of the UK HMSO December 1986

ACTIVITY 6
Study data 9.27.

A   What reason is put forward to suggest why differences in costs, and therefore a comparative advantage exist?

B   Examine data 9.28–9.30.
What evidence can you find to support the Heckscher–Ohlin theory?

9.27
The Heckscher–Ohlin theory

Eli Heckscher, a Swedish economist, developed a theory to explain the pattern of international trade. Published in his home country after the end of the First World War, it received scant attention. His ideas were developed by Bertil Ohlin who argued that profitable trade can take place when countries take advantage of differences in factor endowments. A country relatively well endowed with land resources but a small labour force such as Australia, will produce land-intensive products such as wheat relatively cheaply, but labour-intensive products such as manufactures relatively expensively. Britain however will produce relatively expensive wheat and cheap manufactured goods as it is well endowed with labour relative to land. Australia will tend to produce and export wheat to Britain and import manufactures.

Source: Adapted from International Economics S. Wells Allen and Unwin London 1973

9.28
IMPORTS TO THE UK 1986 (£000)

	JAPAN	NEW ZEALAND
Food and Animals for Food	19,190	319,201
Machinery and Transport	3,732,886	23,807

Source: Overseas Trade Statistics of the UK HMSO December 1986

9.29
Gross non-residential investment in the UK as a percentage of GDP

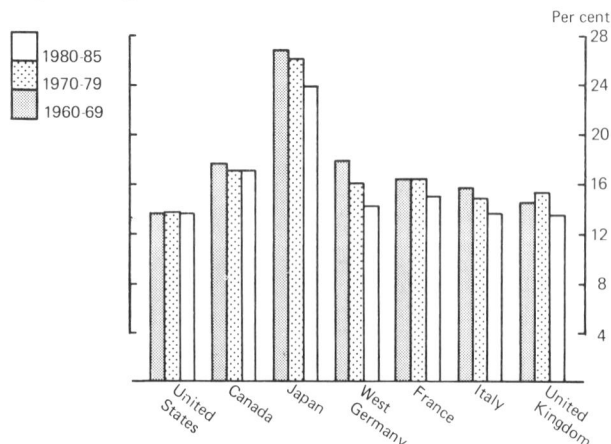

Source: Bank of England Quarterly Bulletin June 1986

9.30
NO SHELTER
The dependence of New Zealand on agriculture dates back to the 1880s when, as part of the Commonwealth, they provided products for the UK. In 1954 Britain took more than 60 per cent of the country's agricultural exports. Today agriculture accounts for 8 per cent of GDP compared to 3 per cent in America and Britain. When associated industries are included, one in five people earn a living from the land. New Zealand, having a small home market (3.2 million people to feed) are dependent on sales of exports.
In 1983, New Zealand accounted for 57 per cent of world trade in sheepmeat, 26 per cent in wool and 18 per cent in butter. The country's limited range of exports leave it open to the effects of price fluctuations. This problem is increased when the relative size of exports to the economy is compared. In New Zealand exports account for 24 per cent of GDP; America's exports account for 6 per cent.

Source: Adapted from The Economist January 18 1986

ACTIVITY 7

A Examine the figures illustrating trade between the UK and India. Use the theories of absolute and comparative advantage, and the findings of the Heckscher–Ohlin theory to explain the pattern of trade which has taken place.

B Within the UK there is regional specialisation in industry and agriculture.
Using the UK as an example explain how the theory of comparative advantage could be applied within a country.

9.31

Trade between the UK and India 1986 (£000)

Items	Value of imports to UK	Value of exports from UK
Food & animals for food	120,047	816
Beverages & tobacco	18,945	3,306
Crude materials (coal, coke, gas, petroleum products, lubricants)	14,077	22,279
Mineral fuel (lubricants)	19,800	5,625
Animal & vegetable products	4,985	79
Chemicals	9,180	58,894
Manufactured goods	110,277	288,131
Textiles	52,741	2,879
Iron & Steel	457	43,882
Machinery & transport equipment	33,331	444,123

Source: *Overseas Trade Statistics of the UK HMSO December 1986*

TASK 4 To evaluate the criticisms of the theory of comparative and absolute advantage.

ACTIVITY 1

The simple example of international trade using two countries and two goods is an example of an economic model. This is a simplified version of reality, which allows economists to make useful predictions about what will happen if variables change. Two simplifying assumptions are:

A Mobility of factors of production within each country.

B Countries specialise and trade in identical (homogeneous) goods. Examine data 9.32 and 9.33. Are the assumptions realistic?

9.32

Migration in the UK

Area	Migrants aged 1 and above within one year of census – area of former residence	Total population on eve of census
North	274,417	3,104,353
Yorks and Humberside	436,456	4,860,484
East Midlands	321,252	3,819,187
East Anglia	162,424	1,871,635
South East	1,530,634	16,795,756
South West	383,950	4,348,908
West Midlands	415,804	5,148,345
North West	538,594	6,414,168

Source: *UK Census 1981*

ACTIVITY 2

Read data 9.34–9.36 explain to a non-economist any possible reasons why countries have a trade advantage, other than comparative costs.

9.33

A powerful indication of the weakness of traditional theory is provided by the phenomenon of intra-industry trade, the simultaneous importing and exporting of products of the same industry, which is estimated to comprise some 60 per cent of trade between developed countries. More fundamentally it reflects the role of intra-industry product-differentiation as a key element in the competitive process. It is no puzzle that the UK should simultaneously import and export whisky of different brands or equally automobiles, given the many grades of product which exist within this commodity group, each model type defined by a unique set of characteristics.

Source: *The UK Economy* Edited by M. J. Artis 11th Edition Weidenfeld and Nicholson London 1986

9.34

The conditions which generate intra-industry trade also make technological innovation an important element in trade performance. Economists have long recognized the connection between technical innovation, technology transfer and changes in the structural pattern of foreign trade. Three factors are recognized as being of proven importance here: time-lags in the inter-country transfer of technology; differences in the national rate of diffusion of innovations; and differences in the rates of growth of national production capacity to exploit innovations. From this perspective, a country's trade performance is determined by the rate at which it acquires and exploits new technologies relative to its major competitors.

Source: *The UK Economy* Edited by M. J. Artis 11th Edition Weidenfeld and Nicholson London 1986

9.36

International competitiveness will depend in part on the kind of factors reflected in the usual relative-price or cost-based measures of competitiveness but it will also depend on a host of less tangible factors. Except in the case of homogeneous products, eg fuels, raw materials and some semi-manufactures, quality and design matter to purchasers as well as price. For capital and other durable goods, delivery dates and after-sales service will be important; for non-durable goods and services it may be reliability and continuity of supply. Effective marketing may also have a significant influence on performance. The term 'non-price competitiveness' has been used to describe these other aspects of competitiveness which, unlike relative prices or costs, are not readily quantified. It seems quite likely that non-price competitiveness is as important as price or cost competitiveness in determining overall performance, but the unquantifiable nature of non-price competitiveness makes this proposition virtually impossible to test. Moreover favourable non-price competitiveness tends to be associated with favourable productivity growth.

Source: *Economic Progress Report* July 1983

9.35

Source: *Sunday Mirror* June 14 1987

ACTIVITY 3

You should now be in a position to evaluate the evidence. Write a passage (as if you were going to read it out) in support of free trade and one in support of protection. If you are working with another student he/she could write the other passage. As a class exercise, divide into two groups and compile a short introduction in support of each argument, followed by an open debate.

SECTION 10 Exchange Rates

HYPOTHESIS	Fluctuations in the value of the pound against other currencies can lead to major problems for the UK economy.

When the price of one currency is expressed in terms of another this is called an exchange rate. Data 10.2 shows fluctuations of the pound sterling against the dollar and the D mark since 1982. The Prime Minister clearly could not understand why the value of the pound was falling in January 1985. However, some commentators have stressed the importance of North Sea oil and UK interest rates (high by international standards) in explaining changes in the sterling exchange rate.

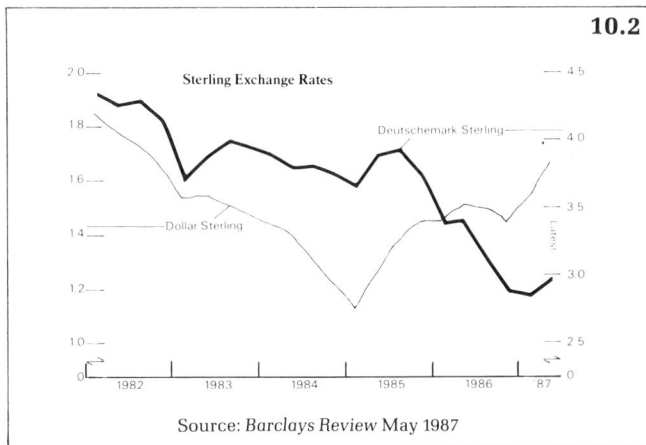

10.1

'It is something of a mystery as to why sterling has been falling.'

Source: The Prime Minister on the Jimmy Young Programme January 1985

'A continuation of the fall in crude oil prices had put the exchange rate down against other leading currencies.'

Source: The *Financial Times* February 5 1986

'Put in an international context, the high level of UK interest rates is even more dramatic.... However, without the interest rate differential the pound would probably fall.'

Source: The *Guardian* November 12 1986

10.2

Sterling Exchange Rates

Source: *Barclays Review* May 1987

TASK 1 To discover the factors which influence the exchange rate.

ACTIVITY 1
Study data 10.2 and 10.3.

A Describe the trends in the sterling/dollar exchange rate.

B Can you find a relationship between changes in the sterling/dollar exchange rate and the difference between UK and US interest rates? If so, what is the relationship?

C Does the relationship also apply when the sterling/D mark exchange rate and the difference between UK and West German interest rates is studied?

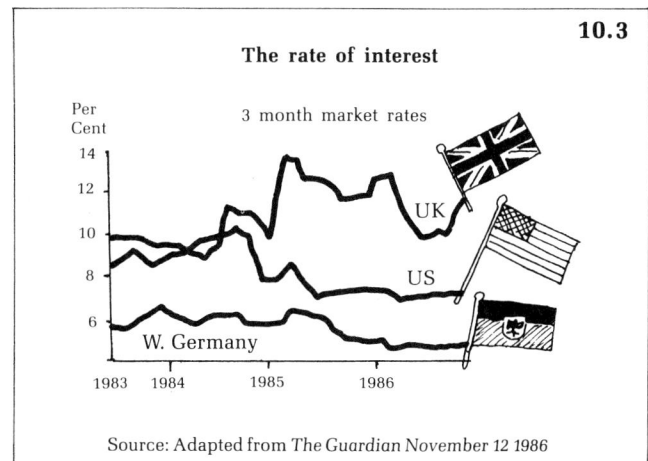

10.3

The rate of interest

Source: Adapted from The *Guardian* November 12 1986

ACTIVITY 2

Before considering the factors which explain fluctuations in exchange rates, it will be remembered that an exchange rate is simply the relative price of two currencies and as with all prices can be studied using demand and supply curves.

In data 10.4 the demand for sterling D is negatively sloped. It depends upon the overseas demand for UK exports of goods and services which are paid for in sterling and the overseas demand for sterling to buy financial assets.

A rise in the sterling exchange rate from £1 = $1 to £1 = $2 will increase the foreign currency price of a UK export, making it less attractive to a foreign buyer. This will generally reduce the demand for pounds on the foreign exchange market.

The supply of sterling S is positively sloped. It depends upon the UK's demand for imported goods and services which are paid for by selling sterling for foreign currency and on the UK's desire to buy foreign financial assets.

A rise in the sterling exchange rate from £1 = $1 to £1 = $2 will reduce the sterling price of a foreign import, making it more attractive in this country. This will generally increase the demand for imported goods and hence the supply of sterling on the foreign exchange market.

In data 10.4 £1 = $1 is a stable equilibrium exchange rate. Any exchange rate above or below this rate will result in market forces pushing the rate back to its equilibrium value, where demand equals supply.

What problems may result if a currency has its value artificially maintained above the equilibrium?

10.4

Exchange Rate Determination

The Foreign Exchange Market

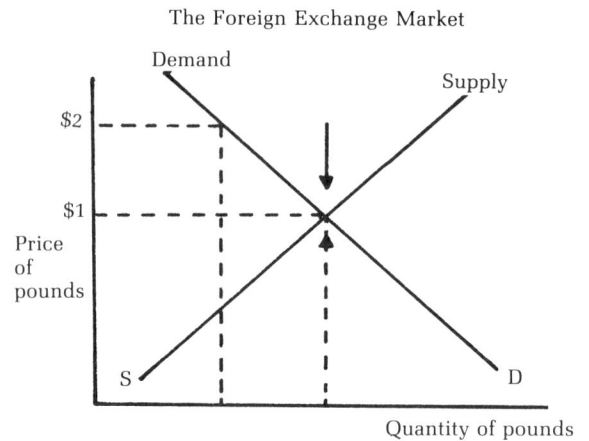

Example
The dollar price of a £20,000 Jaguar car in the USA will depend on the sterling/dollar exchange rate. At £1 = $1 the car will sell for $20,000. However, if the pound rises in value to £1 = $2, the car will cost $40,000 as Americans have to give up twice as many dollars in exchange for each pound. They would normally be expected to buy fewer UK exports.

	Rise in value of £	Fall in value of £
Exchange rate change	£1 = $1 to £1 in $2	£1 = $2 to £1 = $1
Effect on UK exports to America	More expensive Americans pay $2 not $1 for a £1 good	Cheaper Americans pay $1 not $2 for a £1 good
Effect on UK imports from America	Cheaper UK citizens pay 50p not £1 for a $1 good	More expensive UK citizens pay £1 not 50p for a $1 good

ACTIVITY 3

Equilibrium exchange rates are continually disturbed by changes in demand and supply conditions on the foreign exchange market. This is illustrated in data 10.5 and 10.6.

What would be the effect of the following on the demand for, and supply of pounds on the foreign exchange market?

A   Volkswagen introduce a new hatchback capable of 70 mpg at motorway speeds. It only requires a service every 20,000 miles and sells for the price of a Metro.

B   A high rate of economic growth in the American economy increases US demand for British goods.

C   A Japanese compact disc manufacturer launches a very successful advertising campaign in the UK.

D   Sales of UK produced records decrease as British pop music becomes less fashionable in the USA.

Using a separate demand and supply diagram for each of the above, show how a shift in the demand for pounds or the supply of pounds on the foreign exchange market affects the equilibrium exchange rate.

10.5

Effect of an increase in UK demand for imported goods
A marked increase in the UK's demand for Japanese cars would increase the supply of pounds on the foreign exchange market as car importers sell pounds to gain the yen required by the Japanese manufacturer.

This is represented by a rightwards shift in the supply curve of pounds S1 to S2. The impact on the equilibrium exchange rate is to reduce it from ER1 to ER2.

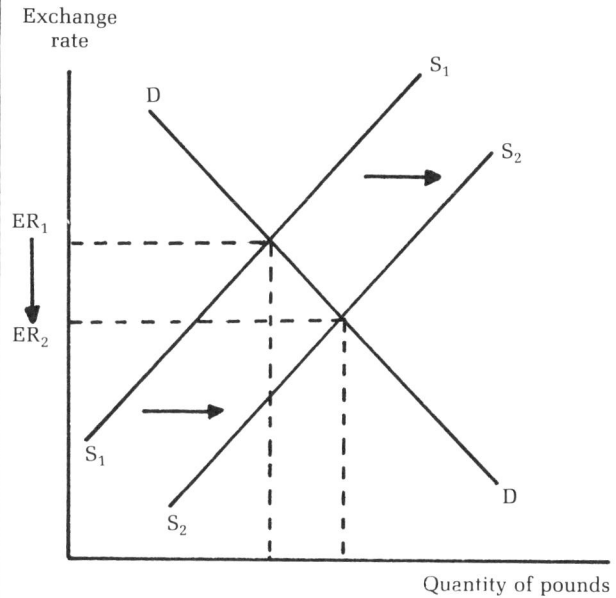

10.6

Effect of an increase in demand for UK exports
A successful buy British campaign held in the USA would raise American demand for British exports and so increase the demand for pounds on the foreign exchange market.

This is represented by a rightwards shift in the demand curve for pounds D1 to D2. The impact on the equilibrium exchange rate is to increase it from ER1 to ER2.

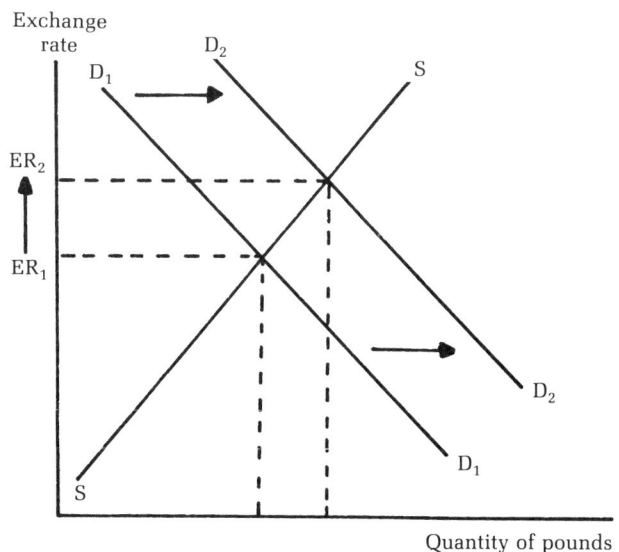

ACTIVITY 4

UK interest rates and sterling.

As data 10.3 shows, UK interest rates are indeed high by international standards. But what is the link between interest rates and the exchange rate?

Investors aiming to maximise their returns compare interest rates in say London, with New York or Tokyo. Other things being equal, a rise in UK interest rates attracts foreign capital, increasing the demand for the pound and raising the exchange rate. In contrast, if US interest rates increase, investors sell pounds and buy dollars, forcing the sterling/dollar exchange rate to fall. The government may have to step in and raise UK interest rates to prevent this fall.

Examine data 10.7 which refers to the sterling collapse of January 1985. Can undesirable movements in the exchange rate always be checked by raising or lowering interest rates? If not, what other factors might be important?

10.7

Sterling's collapse and interest rates...

After two weeks which have seen the pound down by 2.5 per cent, interest rates up by 2.5 per cent and the government's reputation for stern resolve in its handling of the economy in temporary tatters, it is surprising just how many questions there are still left unanswered. For a start, it is not yet clear whether the long-run downward trend in the pound which began at the beginning of 1981 has been decisively checked by the dramatic hike in interest rates. The momentum of that decline is considerable – the pound has fallen nearly 16 per cent since February 1981.

The uncertainty is compounded because it is equally unclear exactly what the government really wants. Thus the question of where interest rates go next is as muddy as the Thames at low tide.

Both the interest rate rise and the Chancellor's statements to the House and press since then have been designed to break the foreign exchange market's psychology. In itself, a 2.5 per cent rise in interest rates cannot stop the slide. If you are a speculator who believes that the pound will, say, lose 10 per cent of its value over the next three months, you are not going to be wildly impressed by the offer of an extra 2.5 per cent over a year. But if the markets believe that the Chancellor will go further – either by raising interest rates again or by organising the sort of support package of official buying of sterling which is the only thing to have stopped really severe runs on the currency in the past, then the irony is that he will not need them. Psychology is all.

Source: Adapted from an article by Christopher Huhne *The Guardian* January 17 1985

ACTIVITY 5

Study data 10.8 and 10.9.

A What impact will a fall in world oil prices have on the sterling exchange rate?

B 'Weak oil market equals weak pound.' Referring to data 10.10 and 10.11, how important is oil in explaining the sterling/dollar exchange rate?

10.9

Dynamic Path of Sterling Following Oil Price Decline

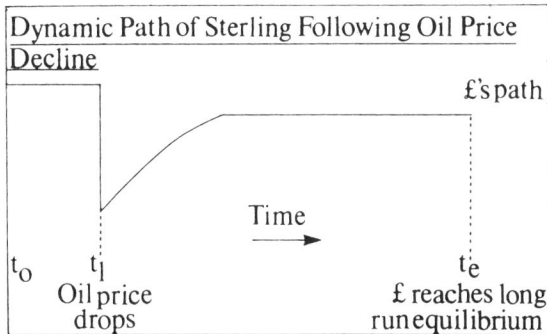

£'s path

Time →

t_0 — Oil price drops

t_1

t_e — £ reaches long run equilibrium

Source: *The International Economic Analyst* Goldman Sachs February 1987

10.8

Oil prices and sterling

Since the beginning of 1985 the dollar price of North Sea Brent crude oil has been as high as $31 per barrel and as low as $8 per barrel. Such swings in oil prices carry implications for exchange rates.

The UK is a net oil exporter since it exports more oil than it imports. A falling world price of oil coupled with a low price elasticity of demand (demand will change little as the price changes), will result in a reduced foreign demand for sterling and, other things being equal, a falling exchange rate.

Recent research suggests that the pound will tend to drop by approximately 3.5 per cent in the long run following a 10 per cent oil price cut.

Lower oil prices reduce the value of UK exports and so worsen the current account of the balance of payments. This will result in a depreciation of sterling which in the long run will stimulate exports, reduce imports and so restore equilibrium to the balance of payments. However, imports and exports take time to respond to a falling exchange rate. The initial effect may be to make the current account deficit even worse. The increase in the supply of sterling and reduced demand on the foreign exchange market will initially result in the value of the pound falling by more than the 3.5 per cent required in response to a 10 per cent oil price decline. This is known as exchange rate overshoot.

In the long run, as trade volumes respond to the lower exchange rate which makes UK exports more competitive in foreign markets and imported goods less attractive in the UK, the exchange rate will recover. This is shown in data 10.9.

10.10

$/$ and oil prices

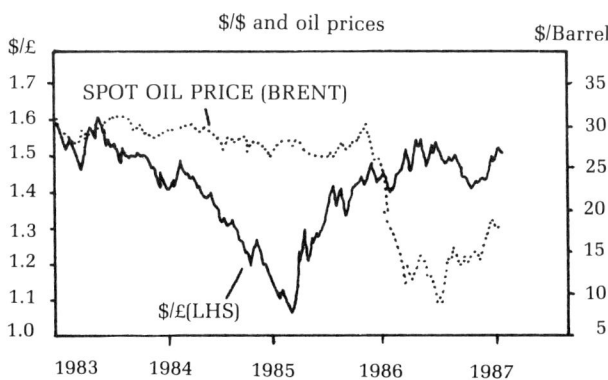

$/£ (left axis) / $/Barrel (right axis)

SPOT OIL PRICE (BRENT)

$/£(LHS)

1983 1984 1985 1986 1987

Source: *The International Economic Analyst* Goldman Sachs February 1987

10.11

The weight of oil 1983 – Britain

Oil output as a percentage of GDP	Net oil exports as a percentage of total exports
6.6%	11.3%

Source: *The Economist* February 2 1985

ACTIVITY 6

The Economist has recently put the PPP theory of exchange rates to the test. Read data 10.12 and the extract which summarises their findings.

A Do the findings in data 10.12 support belief in the Law of One Price or not?

B Outline the limitations of the PPP approach to exchange rates and the use of Big Macs as a measuring stick in particular.

10.12

A purchasing power parity explanation of exchange rate movements

In the long run, many economists believe that currencies will tend towards the exchange rates which result in the same prices being charged for the same goods in different countries. This Law of One Price or purchasing Power Parity (PPP) principle as it is called can be explained simply by an example.

If a Volkswagen Golf of identical specification can be bought in West Germany for £650 less than it can in this country, somebody somewhere will start buying Golfs in West Germany where they are relatively cheap and selling them in this country where they are relatively expensive. Over time, this practice through its impact on supply and demand will eliminate the price differential and result in PPP.

10.13

On the hamburger standard

GOLDEN ARCHES

Depressing though it may be to gourmets, the "Big Mac" hamburger sold by McDonald's could well oust the basket of currencies as an international monetary standard. After all, it is sold in 41 countries, with only the most trivial changes of recipe. That ought to say something about comparative prices. Think of the hamburger as a medium-rare guide to whether currencies are trading at the right exchange rates.

Big-Mac-watchers will rely on the theory of purchasing-power parity (PPP) for currencies. This argues that an exchange rate between two currencies is in equilibrium (ie, at PPP) when it equates the prices of a basket of goods and services in both countries—or, in this case, that rate of exchange which leaves hamburgers costing the same in each country. Comparing actual exchange rates with PPPs is one indication of whether a currency is under- or over-valued.

The Economist's correspondents around the world have been gorging themselves in a bid to test Mac-PPPs. In Washington, a Big Mac costs $1.60; in Tokyo, our *Makudonarudo* correspondent had to fork out Y370 ($2.40).

Dividing the yen price by the dollar price yields a Mac-PPP of $1=Y231; but on September 1st, the dollar's actual exchange rate stood at Y154. The same method gives a Mac-PPP against the D-mark of DM2.66, compared with a current rate of DM2.02. Conclusion: on Mac-PPP grounds, the dollar looks under-valued against the yen and the D-mark.

Sterling is different. The Mac-PPP for the pound is $1.45 (69p to the dollar), within a whisker of the actual rate of around $1.49. But the pound's Mac-PPP against the D-mark is DM3.86, suggesting that sterling is undervalued at DM3.02. British industrialists, who squeal about the pound's current "strength", will now like hamburgers even less.

The Australian dollar appears to have been heavily oversold; it is 34% below its Mac-PPP rate against the American dollar. Meanwhile, the Irish pound seems to be spot on. However, our correspondent in Ireland has uncovered an opportunity for arbitrage. This month, a Big Mac can be enjoyed in Dublin for just 20 tokens from milk cartons.

The hamburger standard provides the

Big MacCurrencies

Hamburger prices round the world

Country	Price* in local currency	Implied† purchasing power parity of the dollar	Actual exchange rate Sept 1st	% over (+) or under (−) valuation of US$
Australia	A$1.75	1.09	1.64	+50
Belgium	BFr90	.56	42	−25
Brazil	Cz$2.5	7.80	13.80	+78
Britain	£1.10	0.69	0.67	−3
Canada	C$1.89	1.18	1.39	+18
France	FFr16.4	10.30	6.65	−35
Hongkong	HK$7.60	4.75	7.80	+64
Ireland	IR£1.18	0.74	0.74	−1
Japan	Y370	231	154	−33
Holland	Fl4.35	2.72	2.28	−16
Singapore	S$2.80	1.75	2.15	+23
Spain	Ptas260	163	133	−18
Sweden	SKr16.5	10.30	6.87	−33
United States	$1.60	—	—	—
W Germany	DM4.25	2.66	2.02	−24

*Source: McDonald's *Prices may vary slightly between branches. †Foreign price divided by dollar price.*

United States with strong evidence for its contention that Asian NICs (newly industrialising countries) ought to upvalue their currencies; they are more or less tied to the dollar, so their exchange rates have barely budged during the past 18 months. A hamburger costs 64% more in Washington than in Hongkong—ie, on Mac-PPP grounds the dollar is 64% over-valued against the Hongkong dollar. It is also 23% too high against the Singapore dollar.

Caveat hamburger

The hamburger standard has its limitations. Using purchasing-power parities to forecast movements in exchange rates can produce misleading results. For instance, price differences between countries can be distorted by taxes, transport costs, property costs or such things as the famously high retail mark-ups in Japan and West Germany.

A more serious objection is that a PPP simply indicates where exchange rates should be in the long run if price levels were the only difference between countries. In fact, there are many other differences. So even though PPPs are handy for converting living standards (GDP per person) into a common currency, they are not necessarily the best way to judge the exchange rate needed to bring the current account of the balance of payments into "equilibrium". Confused? Some economics can be hard to digest.

Currency dealers get younger by the day

Source: *The Economist* September 6–12 1986

TASK 2   To investigate the costs and benefits of a change in the exchange rate.

What Exchange Rate Do We Want – Rising, Falling or Stable?
'There is no such thing as an ideal exchange rate for industry, simply because firms have conflicting interests.'
The quotation above is taken from data 10.15 which discusses the good and bad sides of the sterling collapse of January 1985.

ACTIVITY 1

A   Study data 10.14–10.17 and then compile a list of the advantages and disadvantages associated with
   ● a falling exchange rate and
   ● a rising exchange rate.

B   Despite conflicting interests what similar needs do importers and exporters each have? You could attempt this activity in groups.

10.14

Value of pound falls against other currencies

10.15

The good and bad sides to the collapse

THERE WILL be mixed feelings in the boardrooms of industry over the collapse of sterling.

While all sides of industry will share the disappointment and unease at the latest $2\frac{1}{2}$ point rise in the cost of borrowing, there will be conflicting reactions among exporters and importers about the performance of the pound.

The drop in the value of the pound makes it cheaper for exporting firms to sell British goods in foreign markets particularly America. But the decline also drives up the cost of goods being imported into the country.

Therefore, traditional large-scale exporters like car manufacturers and defence equipment suppliers will be rapturous about sterling's decline. But those who rely heavily on importing foreign raw materials, like food manufacturers and key electronic firms will be concerned at the rising cost of paying for essential supplies.

Importers' concern at sterling's decline has been partly offset by some fall in commodity prices, notably oil and metal prices. But even this has brought only modest relief because many commodities – including oil – are priced in dollars, not pounds.

However, there is no such thing as an ideal exchange rate for industry, simply because firms have conflicting interests.

For example, the Confederation of British Industry, which represents the most authoritative voice of business, has no fixed policy on exchange rates. Stick a pin in the CBI on just about every other industrial issue and the organisation will come up with a clear view.

But on sterling, the CBI's widespread membership is divided between those exporters who want their goods priced more competitively in world markets and those who want their raw materials to cost less. It is a classic difference of opinion.

In an ideal world, industrialists would first and foremost plump for a stable exchange rate, not necessarily a higher or lower one. Companies, both exporters and importers, get incensed at the wild fluctuations in sterling which makes it very difficult to sensibly price long-term overseas development projects or supply contracts. It is a common gripe, but one which politicians down the years have ignored.

Some exporters simply abandoned their attempts to sell British made goods to America when sterling was riding high at 2.40 to the dollar. It was hardly worth the effort.

One method of offsetting the additional costs from sterling's decline against the dollar has been for UK companies to buy firms in America. But this smacks of transferring jobs out of Britain into America at a time when over 3 million Britons are looking for work and does nothing to improve the government's credibility on exchange rate policy.

However, all firms will unite in their opposition to higher interest rates. Each one point increase in banking interest rates adds at least £250 million a year to the annual cost of meeting interest charges on loans, so the $2\frac{1}{2}$ point rise in the past few days will cost industry at least £625 million.

Industry will be particularly upset at the latest rise in interest rates because they come at a time when many firms have been borrowing heavily to pay for more investment in plant and machinery.

Source: *The Guardian* January 15 1985

10.16
The Exchange Rate and Inflation

Calendar Year Averages	US $/£ Exchange Rate	UK Inflation percentage change in Retail Price Index
1983	1.52	4.6
1984	1.33	5.0
1985	1.29	6.1
1986	1.40	3.4

Source: *Bank of England Quarterly Bulletin, Employment Gazette*

10.17

Holidays cheaper as crisis dollar crashes

THE dollar crashed dramatically yesterday, threatening to spark off another worldwide money panic.

But it means cheaper US holidays and it could force the British Government to cut interest rates – making our mortgages and bank loans cost less.

Chancellor Nigel Lawson will want to stop money flowing from America to Britain.

Dearer

That would push the pound even higher, making British exports dearer for Americans to buy.

Yesterday the pound zoomed up by more then three cents to 1.864 dollars – its highest for five years.

The dollar has fallen by a tenth since last October when a run on the dollar sparked the Black Monday crash on Stock Exchanges round the world.

Plunge

City dealers were worried last night that share prices might plunge when the London Stock Exchange opens today.

Shares fell sharply in America, Japan and Europe yesterday.

The dollar crisis stems from worries about vast overspending by the American Government and the States' widening trade gap with the rest of the world.

Source: *The Daily Mirror* December 29 1987

TASK 3 To evaluate the arguments concerning fixed and flexible exchange rates.

ACTIVITY 1
Study data 10.18–10.19.

A What is meant by the term 'sterling crisis'

B How might such a crisis be caused and what measures might the government take to deal with it?

The Foreign Exchange Market

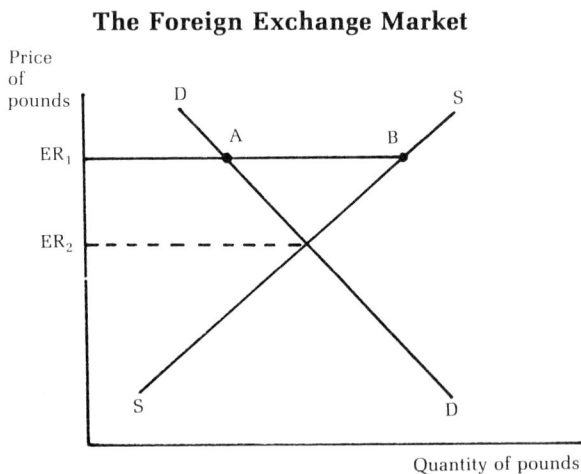

10.18

FIRST A HISTORY LESSON . . . .

From the end of the Second World War to the early 1970s a system of fixed but adjustable exchange rates operated. The Bretton Woods system, as it became known, committed governments to declare and maintain a set rate of exchange between its own currency and others which could only be changed in circumstances of fundamental disequilibrium in the balance of payments.

During the 1960s there were a number of sterling crises. As governments attempted to boost output and employment by implementing Keynesian demand management policies, the balance of payments deteriorated as higher domestic demand sucked in imports and redirected export production to the home market. This reduced the demand for sterling and increased its supply on the foreign exchange market and hence put downward pressure on the exchange rate.

Consider the foreign exchange market diagram. The government sought to maintain the exchange rate above its equilibrium value at ER1 by interest rate manipulation and foreign exchange market intervention. To this end, the Bank of England would buy pounds equal to the distance A–B and pay for them by running down its foreign currency reserves. Clearly, this could not be sustained indefinitely as foreign exchange reserves would be quickly depleted. In the longer term, solutions included deflating demand in the economy and/or devaluing the currency to ER2, which equates demand and supply in the foreign exchange market.

Critics of the Bretton Woods system argued that by allowing markets to set exchange rates rather than governments, these crises would be avoided. When the Bretton Woods system collapsed in the early 1970s, Britain was one of the leading powers that adopted flexible exchange rates.

10.19

STOP PRESS . . . . . STOP PRESS . . . .
Sterling fell back heavily on the foreign exchanges this morning
when the Bank of England announced a closing down
sale . . . .

ACTIVITY 2

Study data 10.20–10.24. Do the major criticisms
levelled at flexible exchange rates appear
justified? Explain your answer using examples
from the data.

10.20

Have floating exchange rates proved successful?

The move to market determined exchange rates has, according to
many economists, created more problems than it has solved.

The major charges levelled against the floating rate system are:

1. Currencies have fluctuated greatly and this is damaging to the
   growth of world trade and investment because the
   uncertainty involved raises the risk of undertaking
   international business.
2. Even more seriously, exchange rates have moved away from
   their equilibrium values for long and damaging periods.
   These large and prolonged currency misalignments represent
   a threat to free trade as they have resulted in large trade
   imbalances and calls for protectionist measures. The impact
   of the dollar's appreciation between 1980 and 1985 on the US
   trade balance is shown in data 10.21.
3. Large and sustained currency appreciations result in
   employment losses.

10.21

Exchange Rate Volatility

(Standard deviation expressed as a percentage of the weekly
nominal exchange rate around its six-months [27 week] moving
average)

EXCHANGE RATES AGAINST THE US DOLLAR

	1974	1975	1976	1977	1978	1979	1980	1981	1982	1983	1984	1985*
Yen	2.34	0.91	1.03	1.60	2.93	2.22	3.18	2.31	3.15	2.01	1.56	2.17
Deutschemark	2.88	2.13	0.97	1.12	2.18	1.36	2.60	3.15	2.05	1.82	2.52	2.78
French franc	2.21	2.18	1.09	0.61	1.75	1.31	2.40	2.62	2.79	1.94	2.44	2.79
Pound sterling	1.83	1.29	2.52	0.85	2.10	2.49	1.87	2.43	1.38	2.00	1.87	3.87
Italian lira	1.92	1.75	3.11	0.20	1.31	1.17	2.43	2.18	2.09	1.59	2.21	2.35
Canadian dollar	0.47	0.48	0.98	0.83	1.03	1.02	1.04	0.82	1.18	0.29	0.70	1.03
Belgian franc	2.55	1.95	1.03	1.03	2.24	1.49	2.57	2.86	2.67	1.64	2.51	2.75
Dutch guilder	2.43	1.95	1.07	0.97	2.19	1.44	2.51	3.09	1.75	1.72	2.50	2.81
Swedish krona	2.45	2.06	0.90	2.35	1.19	0.92	1.81	1.57	3.77	1.06	1.75	2.10
Swiss franc	2.67	2.13	0.79	1.07	4.09	1.68	3.15	3.51	2.30	1.91	2.10	3.38

Source: *The International Economist Analyst* Goldman Sachs February
1987

10.22

TRADE BALANCES
seasonally adjusted annual rates, CIF valuation

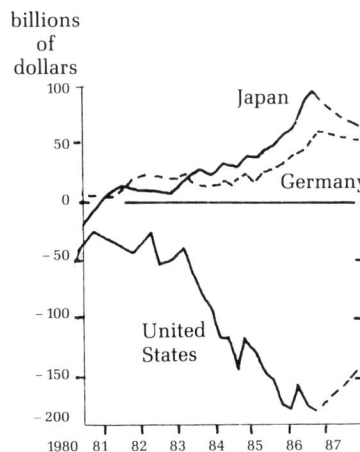

Source: *World Financial Markets* February/March 1987

10.23

UK Unemployment 1973–1986

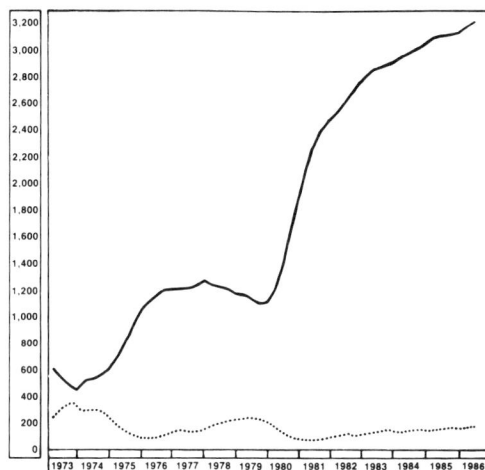

Source: *Employment Gazette* September 1986

10.24

Sterling/Dollar Exchange Rate
1977–86 (Annual Averages)

YEAR	1977	1978	1979	1980	1981	1982	1983	1984	1985	1986
£	1·7455	1·9197	2·1225	2·3281	2·0254	1·7489	1·5158	1·3364	1·2976	1·4672

Source: Bank of England Quarterly Bulletin, *Employment News*

ACTIVITY 3

Data 10.25 illustrates how the joint support arrangements which would always be on offer if sterling joined the ERM of the EMS stemmed the fall of the pound against the D-mark in October 1986.

A   Read the text in data 10.25 and then study data 10.26. Explain how sterling might benefit from full membership of the EMS.

B   What problems might the UK encounter if sterling joins the ERM?

10.25

EMS option for sterling

Experience of the problems associated with flexible exchange rates have led some to favour a return to more managed rates. In particular, some economists support the case for sterling's admission to the Exchange Rate Mechanism (ERM) of the European Monetary System EMS.

The EMS was formed in March 1979 with the intention of creating a zone of monetary stability in Europe. Great emphasis has been placed on its ERM which sets limits on the admissable movements in the currencies of the member countries against each other. Should these limits be breached, action by the member states' central banks would stem the fall or rise and so push the exchange rate back within its limits. This would be achieved by buying or selling currency on the foreign exchange market.

10.26

Bank of England and Bundesbank co-operate to save the pound . . . . . .

The Bank of England entered the foreign exchange market yesterday. It bought pounds with its foreign currency reserves to prevent the pound from falling further. However, it was unable to stem the flow of money out of sterling and three month money market interest rates climbed from 10.5 per cent to 11.25 per cent.

With the Bank of England on the point of defeat, West Germany's Bundesbank – its central bank – intervened. It began to sell D-marks for pounds. The increased demand for pounds on the international exchanges raised sterling's value, avoided the need for UK interest rates to rise and illustrated how Britain might benefit from the joint support actions which would be permanently available if sterling joined the ERM of the EMS.

Proponents of the EMS argue that if sterling belonged to the ERM, UK interest rates would tend to fall to the European average. This would enhance employment prospects in Britain as national output would be stimulated by lower interest rates. Moreover, by closely tying the value of the pound to the D-mark, UK inflation would fall to the relatively low rates experienced in West Germany. Supporters also argue that full EMS membership, ie a commitment to stabilise sterling's value against other EMS currencies would provide discipline in wage negotiations. If a trade union negotiated a wage increase in excess of productivity improvements, it would make British goods less competitive in overseas markets and so increase unemployment amongst its own members.

Critics of the EMS make the point that joint central bank intervention does not always work. They argue that government power in the foreign exchange markets is fragile in that interventions can be swamped by changes in market sentiment. A run on the pound could either result in Britain's hasty exit from the EMS or cause greater variability in UK interest rates.

Moreover, full EMS membership would only stabilise sterling's value against other EMS currencies. It would not prevent the

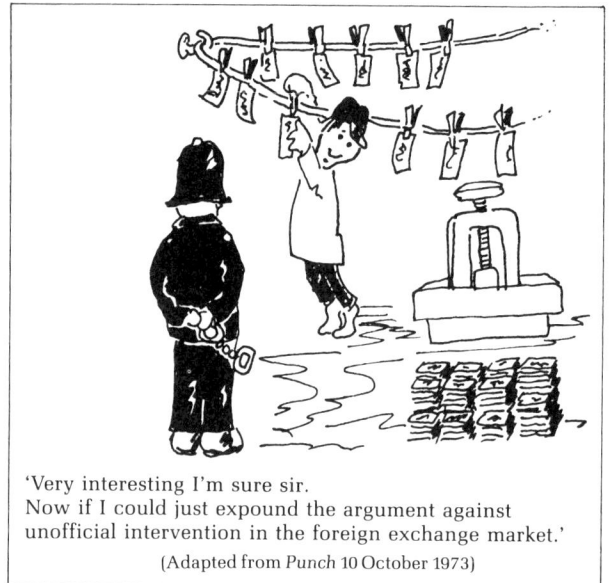

'Very interesting I'm sure sir.
Now if I could just expound the argument against unofficial intervention in the foreign exchange market.'

(Adapted from *Punch* 10 October 1973)

pound's excessive fluctuations against non-EMS currencies such as the dollar and yen. What is needed is a global reform package, not one solely based on Europe.

Source: Adapted from an article by Christopher Smallwood The *Sunday Times* October 5 1986